Creating Curriculum Using Children's Picture Books

by
Kelly Gunzenhauser and Sherrill B. Flora

illustrated by
Chris Olsen

Publisher
Key Education Publishing Company, LLC
Minneapolis, Minnesota

CONGRATULATIONS ON YOUR PURCHASE OF A KEY EDUCATION PRODUCT!

The editors at Key Education are former teachers who bring experience, enthusiasm, and quality to each and every product. Thousands of teachers have looked to the staff at Key Education for new and innovative resources to make their work more enjoyable and rewarding. Key Education is committed to developing and publishing educational materials that will assist teachers in building a strong and developmentally appropriate curriculum for young children.

PLAN FOR GREAT TEACHING EXPERIENCES WHEN YOU USE
EDUCATIONAL MATERIALS FROM KEY EDUCATION PUBLISHING COMPANY, LLC

Credits
Authors: Kelly Gunzenhauser and Sherrill B. Flora
Publisher: Sherrill B. Flora
Creative Director: Annette Hollister-Papp
Illustrator: Chris Olsen
Editor: Karen Seberg
Production: Key Education Staff
Cover Photo Credits: © Shutterstock.com

Key Education welcomes manuscripts and product ideas from teachers.
For a copy of our submission guidelines, please send a self-addressed, stamped envelope to:

Key Education Publishing Company, LLC
Acquisitions Department
9601 Newton Avenue South
Minneapolis, Minnesota 55431

To Eric, who loves to read, and Casey, who loves to be read to.

–KG

About the Author

Kelly Gunzenhauser has a master's degree in English and taught writing at the college level. She has been an editor and writer in the educational publishing field for over nine years, as well as a volunteer for public schools. Kelly is the mother of a toddler and a volunteer for his preschool.

Standard Book Number: 978-1-602680-11-1
Creating Curriculum Using Children's Picture Books
Copyright © 2008 by Key Education Publishing Company, LLC
Minneapolis, Minnesota 55431

Contents

Introduction

Regardless of what trends and new research show, exposure to literature remains one of the most important components of early childhood education. There is nothing quite like a really good book to capture children's interest and help fuel their desire to read independently. But, a love for reading is only a small part of why children's literature should be used in the classroom. Children's books are delightfully flexible and imaginative. Just from encountering the small sample of literature explored in this book, children can learn about the moon, worms, ducklings, kindergarten, snow, and fairy tales. They can share in the experience as characters find a friend, achieve a goal, learn through trial and error, entertain a guest, negotiate an agreement, and care for a pet. They can learn simple words such as *dog*, *big*, and *bell* or complicated vocabulary such as *neutral*, *collecting*, and *escalator*.

With such a wealth of resources available, it seems only natural to build curriculum around children's books. Children's books touch on every possible subject, theme, and skill teachers could possibly want to teach, including motor skills, rhythm and music, science, math, art, social studies, problem solving, creative dramatics, manners and social skills, and, of course, reading and language arts. All educators of young children want to teach at least some of these skills, but finding the context in which to naturally teach them can be difficult. Children's literature helps teachers build organic learning situations in the classroom. Teachers can find a context for all manner of art projects, games, fine and gross motor activities, social studies activities, math activities, creative dramatics activities, and social skills activities by connecting them to children's books.

It may seem old-fashioned, but it really is smart to base young children's education on children's literature. As a teacher, it feels good to pull out books you love—or discover new classics—and share them with your students. As a child, it makes sense to create art projects, do experiments, play games, build structures, and learn words that revolve around a familiar tale and beloved characters. So, dust off your books, sit in a circle, read the stories, and prepare to inspire a roomful of learning and fun.

Bears

Written by Ruth Krauss
Illustrated by Maurice Sendak
Copyright 2005
HarperCollins

Story Summary

In the original version of this story, illustrator Phyllis Rowand used straightforward depictions of bears performing various actions. Sendak takes a more adventurous approach by showing the rivalry between a boy's favorite stuffed bear and his jealous dog. Fans of Sendak's *Where the Wild Things Are* will find the boy—who is dressed in a wolf suit—very familiar.

Themes:
- emotions
- problem solving
- perseverance

Skills:
- phonemic awareness
- position words
- quantity words
- measurement
- biology
- scissor skills
- balance
- sequencing

Vocabulary:
collecting, everywhere, fares, millionaires, stares, washing

Related Books:
Corduroy
by Don Freeman
(Viking, 1968)

The Velveteen Rabbit
by Margery Williams
(Doubleday, 1958)

Before the Story

Look at the book's cover and ask children what they think this book will be about. Ask how many of them have stuffed bears or other animals. Then, ask how many of them have pets. Do their pets ever bother their stuffed animals? Do their pets have stuffed animals or toys of their own? How do their pets play with their toys?

During the Story

Reinforce each action by acting out the story as you read it. Pretend to walk up stairs and look under your own chair. Pantomime washing your hair, staring, collecting money, and so on. It is helpful to place this book on an easel to make the actions easier to perform while reading. Let children respond by performing the actions, as well. This will reinforce their understanding of the new vocabulary words.

After the Story

Reread the story but pause to show all of the places where bears are hidden on each page (the wallpaper, the posts on the staircase, the moon outside the window, the shower curtain, and so on).

Language Arts Connections

Rhyming Words

Help children recognize rhyming words. Reread the book. Tell children to "Grrr!" like a bear when they hear words that rhyme with *bears*. Children may also take turns suggesting words they think rhyme with *bears*. Have classmates respond with a "Grrr!" to all words that have the correct rhyme.

Position Words

Work on position words. Place a stuffed bear in a small chair and ask, "Where is the bear?" Children should answer either in or on the chair (although over there or in front of would also work).

Place the bear in other positions and repeat the question. Children should correctly answer under, next to, beside, or near. Make a set of position cards to play a variety of games. Photograph the bear in, on, under, etc., the chair. Then, write each position word on the back of its photograph.

Math Connections

Few/Many

Ask children to bring in toy bears or use bear manipulatives. Provide an adult-sized chair or beanbag. Place two bears in the chair and ask, "Are there a few bears or many bears in the chair?" Add all of the bears to the chair and repeat the question.

Continue this activity with one and some. Then, compare more and fewer bears and ask questions using numbers, as well.

How Big Is the Bear?

Draw the outline of a standing grizzly bear on a large sheet of butcher paper. The average height is about 7' (2 m). Let children paint the bear brown. Fill in details like facial features and claws. Post the bear next to a bulletin board. Let children measure, mark, and label each other's heights on the bulletin board next to the bear. Then, help children subtract their heights from the bear's height. They should convert their heights from feet and inches into inches and then subtract the inches from 84.

Science Connections

Real Bears

Talk about real bears. What do they eat? Where do they live? How big do they get? Share some bear facts from child-friendly books such as the Wild Bears! series title *Grizzly Bear* by Jason and Jody Stone (Blackbirch Press, 2000) or *Wild Bears* by Seymour Simon (Chronicle Books, 2002).

Hibernation

Do some classroom hibernating. Explain that in the fall, certain animals eat extra food in order to gain fat. The extra fat helps keep them warm and nourished through the winter. Bear mothers often find dens, where they snuggle with their cubs and doze all winter until it is warm enough for food to be plentiful. Simulate the experience by having children snuggle in "dens" just after lunch. Hang blankets from clotheslines or over desks. Dim the lights, play soft music, and let children "hibernate" for a while. Then, wake them with lights, a recording of singing birds, and snacks and drinks.

Problem-Solving and Social Skills Connections

Hide the Bear

Children often lose things and do not know how to begin looking for them. Teach a lesson in finding lost objects. Explain that Max, the boy in the story, has to look everywhere to find where his dog has taken his bear—even silly places like on a train and in a giant bathtub. But, Max perseveres and finds both of them.

Show a stuffed bear to a child and then ask her to leave the room. Hide the bear. Invite her to come back in and find the bear, without other children telling her where it is. Let her take her time looking around the room until she finds it. Allow a few other children a turn to do this, as well. Then, discuss tips for finding lost objects or ways to prevent them from being lost, such as: Look in each area thoroughly. Put things in the same place each time you are done using them. Keep stuffed animals out of your dog's reach, etc.

Fine Motor Connections

Stuffed Bears

Even children as old as second and third graders need practice cutting with scissors. Have children cut out copies of the Dog and Stuffed Bear Patterns (page 8) to use with the second Creative Dramatics Connections activity (below right). Children may also color the patterns for additional fine motor skills practice.

Tickets

If you plan to do the Creative Dramatics Connections train activity (below right), make it more realistic for children by purchasing a roll of raffle tickets. Give lengths of raffle tickets to children and ask them to separate the tickets into pairs. As each child plays conductor, let him tear each passenger's pair of tickets into two separate tickets. Children can later sort the tickets into numerical order for more fine motor work and for practice with counting.

Gross Motor Connections

Careful Where You Walk

Use this activity to help improve children's balance and encourage them to move with precision. Talk about the picture on the pages with the words "Stepping in squares." Discuss to see if children understand that the bears are trying not to step on sidewalk cracks. (Children may mention the familiar rhyme "Step on a crack, break your mother's back.") Then, take children outside to walk on the sidewalk and challenge them to try to step in squares while not stepping on any sidewalk cracks. To make the activity more difficult, use sidewalk chalk to draw additional "cracks" on the sidewalk.

Art Connections

Bear Decorations

Show the drawing of Max's room found at the end of the story and talk about how everything is decorated with bears—the curtains, wallpaper, and even the moon outside are bearlike. Make a replica of Max's room. Provide a large cardboard box. Cut out a hole for a window. (Or, cover a corner of the room with butcher paper and draw a window on the paper.) Add a doll's bed and a shoe box for a bedside table. Use art supplies to decorate the "room" with bears. Children can draw bears on the walls for the very "beary" wallpaper and put a lampshade on a toy bear to create the bear lamp. Make a bear stamp from a bear-shaped manipulative and let children stamp paint on scraps of white fabric or paper to make curtains. Finally, decorate a paper plate like a yellow moon with a bear face and staple it to show through the window. Stock the room with a pillow, a stuffed dog, and a few stuffed bears and let children pretend to be Max, his dog, and the bears.

Creative Dramatics Connections

Ride the Train

Because this book was originally published in 1948, some references may be unfamiliar. For many children outside of urban environments, the concept of traveling by train may be new. Place classroom chairs in two rows and have children sit in the chairs. Play a recording of train noises and act as the train's conductor. Collect tickets and let children bounce up and down as they pretend to ride the train. Encourage them to walk around in the train, but make sure that they walk as if they are in a fast-moving, swaying train car.

Hide the Animals

Talk about all of the places where Max tries to catch his dog and rescue his stuffed bear. Copy a Dog and Stuffed Bear Pattern (page 8) for each child and let them color the pictures. After the end of the day, hide patterns around the classroom for students to find in the morning. Play upbeat music as children race around, imagining they are trying to find their dogs and bears.

Dog and Stuffed Bear Patterns

Directions are found on page 7.

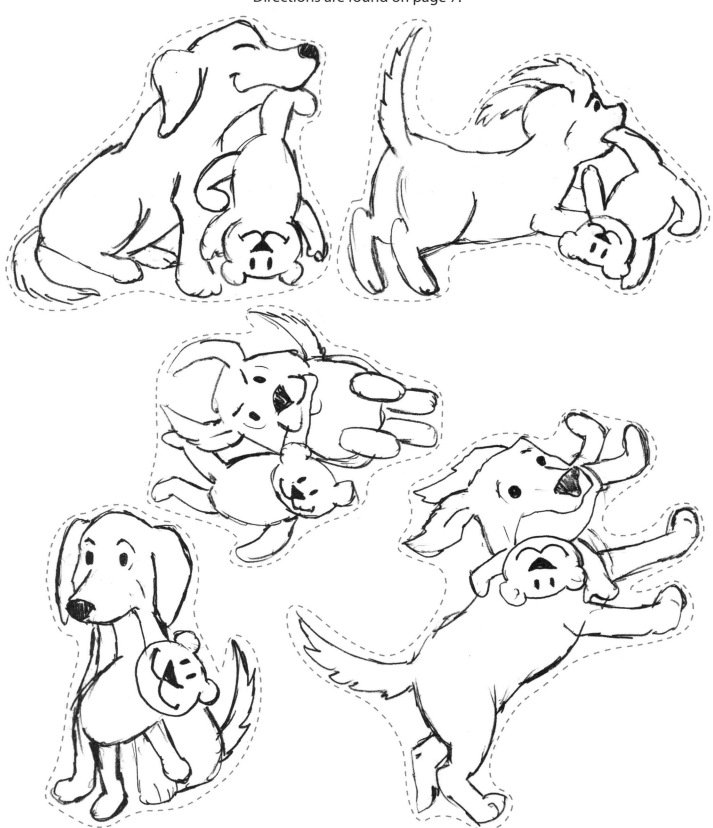

What Happens Next?

Directions: Color the pictures and cut them out out. Put the pictures in the same order as they happened in the story.

CLICK, CLACK, MOO: Cows That Type

Written by Doreen Cronin
Illustrated by Betsy Lewin
Copyright 2000
Simon & Schuster Children's Publishing

Story Summary

Farmer Brown is beside himself when his cows send a typed demand for electric blankets. When the chickens join the cows on strike, he finally agrees to exchange electric blankets for the typewriter, and his farm functions again. Unfortunately for Farmer Brown, he did not bargain on Duck keeping the typewriter.

The author of this child's introduction to strikes, mediation, and neutral parties is also an attorney.

Themes:
- compromising
- negotiating
- farm animals

Skills:
- animal noises
- letter writing
- measurement (temperature)
- typing skills

Vocabulary:
background, believe, demand, electric, exchange, furious, impatient, impossible, meeting, neutral, sincerely, snoop, strike, ultimatum

Related Books:
Giggle, Giggle, Quack by Doreen Cronin (Simon & Schuster, 2002)

Duck for President by Doreen Cronin (Simon & Schuster, 2004)

Before the Story

This book is very appealing to children because of its grown-up theme and the complex vocabulary used to tell a story of a silly situation. Before reading, review all of the vocabulary carefully, as the humor will be lost on children if they are not able to understand the funny words. Also, ask if anyone has ever been to a farm that has cows and chickens and ducks. If so, ask children to guess what the cows might want to do with a typewriter. Would it be very easy for cows to type? Why or why not?

During the Story

Pause as needed while reading to remind children of the meanings of the vocabulary words but be careful not to ruin the flow of the story. As children become familiar with the repeating words *Click, clack, moo. Click, clack, moo. Clickety, clack, moo.*, let them add the "moo" after you say the other words in each phrase.

After the Story

Stop reading before you reach the very last page of the book and talk about whether you think the ducks will get their diving board. Let children explain why they think the ducks will get the board or why they think Farmer Brown may decide he will no longer negotiate with his animals. Then, reveal the last page to solve the mystery.

Language Arts Connections

Animal Noises

Most children love animal noises. After reading this book, also consider reading other books with animal noises, such as *The Noisy Farm* by Marni McGee (Bloomsbury, 2004) or *Quiet Night* by Marilyn Singer (Clarion, 2002). As you read the books and children become familiar with them, let children make the animal noises. Ask what other animal noises children can make, such as pigs oinking, dogs barking, cats meowing, geese honking, sheep baaing, and horses neighing.

meow •
moo •
quack •
cluck •

Language Arts Connections

Note Writing

This book is a perfect introduction to informal note writing. Work with small groups in the language arts center. Ask each child in the group to think of something she would like. You may offer realistic examples, such as extra playground time, a pizza party, or a field trip. Children will then write or dictate their requests to you. First, tell them how to address you in the note. Next, they must state a problem, or reason for the request, and then propose a solution. Have them close the notes with "Sincerely" and sign them. Choose a few requests that you are able to honor and write a note back to the entire class explaining what you will do for them. If children are old enough to negotiate, tell them in writing that you will grant the requests in exchange for their hard work in learning the meanings of the vocabulary words in this book! Then, work with them on the new words and honor their requests as they succeed.

Math Connections

Give a Cow a Blanket

Copy page 14 for each child. Tell children to count the number of flowers next to each cow. Let children give each cow a blanket by cutting out and gluing the correctly numbered blanket on each cow to match that cow's number of flowers.

Problem-Solving and Social Skills Connections

What Do the Other Animals Want?

Talk about the plight of Farmer Brown. Ask if children think his demand of milk and eggs, as a farmer, is unreasonable. Then, ask children if they think the cows' demand for blankets to stay warm is unreasonable. Explain that writing a letter is sometimes a good way to explain what you want and need. Let each child choose another farm animal, such as a horse, pig, cat, dog, chicken, sheep, or goose. Tell children to think of something the animals they have chosen might want from Farmer Brown. Have children write or dictate letters to the farmer telling what they want and giving their reasons why. Then, let children draw pictures of the animals they chose with the objects they requested, as if Farmer Brown has granted their requests.

"Dear Farmer Brown, I would like . . ."

Fine Motor Connections

Old Typewriters

If you have access to old typewriters or to any kind of keyboards, place these on a table in the classroom. Let children practice their typing skills. It is better if the typewriters actually work and the keyboards are connected to computers and monitors so that children can see letters as they type them. You may want to give children some pointers for typing, such as where to place their fingers or how to create spaces or capital letters. Give children some practice words to type, such as *farmer*, *cow*, *hen*, *duck*, etc.

Farm Stick Puppets

Copy page 13 for each child. Children should color the figures, cut them out, and attach them with tape to craft sticks. Children can use the puppets to retell the story of *Click, Clack, Moo: Cows That Type* or use the puppets to make up new animal stories.

Gross Motor Connections

Duck Diving

Review the last three pages of the book, where the ducks ask for (and presumably receive) a diving board. Ask if anyone has ever jumped off a diving board. If so, let those children describe what kinds of jumps or dives they did. Talk about why a diving board would make a pond more exciting. Take children to an open space and provide a low platform, such as a heavy wooden box or milk crate. Place it in a grassy area or one covered with mulch and let children pretend to be the ducks as they jump off the diving board. (Instruct them NOT to dive!) Let each child land in the "water," pretend to swim back to shore, and get back in line to jump off the diving board again.

Art Connections

Giant Cows

Let children make artwork that will contribute to your dramatic play area. On a low bulletin board, draw two large cows in profile. Let children paint the cows with white paint. Then, let them dip sponges into black paint and add black spots to the cows. Staple paper strips around the cows to enclose them in a "barn" and staple strips of construction paper "straw" to the bottom of the board. Then, add the materials suggested in the Creative Dramatics Connections activity (right).

Watercolors

The art style in the book is almost like a coloring book with black, bold outlining strokes filled in with watercolor. Let children draw scenes from the book or other farm scenes and then use watercolors instead of coloring them with crayons. You may want to let children wear smocks and draw their scenes with permanent markers so that the marker strokes do not run when they use the watercolor paints.

Creative Dramatics Connections

A "Real" Pretend Cow

Create a small "working" farm in your classroom. First, create some udders. Fill the fingers and palms of two latex or rubber gloves with fine sand, gelatin, or water. (Double layer the gloves if using water.) Secure the openings of the gloves with rubber bands and staple the tops of the gloves below the bulletin board cows created in the Art Connections activity (left). Use enough staples to firmly anchor the gloves to the bulletin board, being careful not to puncture the filled parts of the gloves. Next, let children create "nests" from shoe boxes and plastic grass or straw. Place the nests on a table next to the bulletin board and fill them with plastic eggs. Provide baskets and pails and let children pretend to be Farmer Brown milking the cows and gathering eggs.

Caution: Before completing this activity, ask families about possible latex allergies.

Farm Stick Puppets

Directions: Color, cut out, and attach each animal and the farmer to a craft stick.

Creating Curriculum Using Children's Picture Books - 13 -

Name _____

Give a Cow a Blanket

Directions: Count the number of flowers next to each cow. Then, read the numbers on the blankets. Cut out each blanket and glue it on the cow that is next to that same number of flowers.

Clifford The Big Red Dog

Written and illustrated
by Norman Bridwell
Copyright 1985, Scholastic Inc.

Story Summary

This story is the beginning of an extensive series. Emily Elizabeth owns a huge, red dog named Clifford. He bumbles through life like most dogs, chasing cars (and catching them), playing with his owner, and being a good boy. While there is very little plot in this story, children will be intrigued by this enormous pet and will probably enjoy reading more stories about Clifford.

Themes:
- pets
- family
- responsibility
- problem solving

Skills:
- adjectives
- counting
- graphing
- classifying

Vocabulary:
anymore, beg, habits, matter, mistakes, perfect, problem, reddest, sometimes, spotted, together, watchdog

Related Books:
Clifford's Birthday Party by Norman Bridwell (Scholastic, 1988)

Clifford's Bedtime by Norman Bridwell (Scholastic, 1991)

Before the Story

Ask for a show of hands from dog owners in the class. Then, ask children who have dogs to show how tall the dogs are by holding their hands parallel to the ground at their dogs' heights. Explain that you are going to read a story about a dog that is more than twice as tall as his owner! Ask children what kinds of problems they think the girl in the story might have owning a dog as big as this. What might be good about owning such a large dog? List all of the good things and bad things that children think might happen in the book.

During the Story

As you read the story, explain any vocabulary words children may have trouble with, especially *mistakes*, *matter*, *problem*, and *watchdog*. On the pages where Clifford is doing a typical "doggy" thing that is made unusual because of his size, stop and ask children about it. For example, ask, "What happened when Clifford decided to chew on a shoe? Is that a regular shoe? What is he doing?"

After the Story

Go back through the list of possible problems that children made before reading the story. Draw a line through any that did not happen and put a check mark by those that did. Explain to children that thinking about what might happen in a book is called *predicting*. Further explain that predicting what might happen in a book will help them decide whether or not they are interested in the story and if they want to read the book.

Predictions

✔ 1. He might not fit in a doghouse.

✔ 2. He would eat a lot of food.

3. ~~He would step on things that he should not step on.~~

✔ 4. You could ride him.

Language Arts Connections

Describing Words

If the children in your classroom are old enough, introduce adjectives. (You may want to call them describing words.) There are many words in the story that describe dogs. Reread the book and have children raise their hands when they hear a word that describes a dog. They should identify *big, red, biggest, reddest, good, small, black, white, brown,* and *spotted.* To tailor this activity to younger children, keep the focus on words that describe color.

Read More Clifford Books

Once children become attached to a character, that familiarity can be a great motivator for them to do more reading. Provide additional books about Clifford in the language arts center for children to read. Help them recognize words that appear throughout the series by posting a word wall in the center with words such as *Clifford, Emily Elizabeth, red, dog,* and others as you and children discover them.

Math Connections

Counting Dogs

For a simple math activity, look at each page and count the dogs in the book besides Clifford. For young children, count consecutively. For older children, write the number of dogs per page, wherever they are found, and then add the numbers.

$$(2 + 2 + 2 + 8 = 14 \text{ dogs})$$

Dog Bone Graph

Copy the Dog Bone Patterns (page 18) to graph information about children's dogs. Draw a bar graph on the board or use a pocket chart. Add headings that match the kind of graph you want to make. To graph the number of dogs per child, ask children with no dogs to raise their hands, then one dog, then two dogs, etc., and attach the corresponding number of bones to the graph. If older children are familiar with dog breeds, ask them to tell you the breeds of dog they own and graph the results.

Science Connections

Classifying

Classification is an important science skill. Teach classification using children's pets. Place several shoe box lids on tables and make a picture sign for each. One lid will hold dog pictures, one will hold cat pictures, etc. (For non-pet-owning children, label a lid "Stuffed Animals.") Ask children to bring in pictures of their pets. Children who do not have pets may bring in pictures of stuffed animals or of pets they would like to have. Help the children write their names, the names of the pet, and the kinds of pets on the backs of their pictures, Then, let the children place their pictures into the correct lids. Check to see that children have sorted their pictures correctly and review each of the animals in the lids with the whole class. Finally, gather all of the pictures together in a large, resealable plastic bag. Place the lids in one area and let children take turns sorting all of the class pets.

Problem-Solving and Social Skills Connections

Solve a Clifford Problem

Take a picture walk through the book and talk about the problems that come with owning Clifford. He catches a car and a policeman, he needs a very big house and a lot of food, and he scares other animals and digs up trees. These problems, with the exceptions of no longer visiting the zoo and having a giant house, are left unresolved. Ask children what it means to be a responsible pet owner. Let each child choose a problem found in the book and write, dictate, or draw how they would solve it. For example, a child who chooses the scenario of Clifford digging up trees could solve the problem by writing a story about having Clifford dig more holes and then planting new trees in their place. A child who wonders how she would feed a dog as big as Clifford could draw a picture of Clifford working at a dog food factory as the official taster. Post the drawings on a bulletin board with a red background.

Fine Motor Connections

Dog Collars

Buckling is a great fine motor skill that many children have little practice with since most shoes are fastened with laces or hook-and-loop tape. Gather stuffed dogs in a variety of sizes and provide as many dog collars as possible. Let children take turns fastening the dog collars on the stuffed dogs. Also, provide leashes for children to snap on the collars. When children have mastered buckling the collars and attaching the leashes, move the materials to the dramatic play area.

Matching Dogs Activity

Copy page 19 for each child. Have children draw lines to match each dog with its owner.

Gross Motor Connections

Hide and Seek

Most children love a good game of hide and seek! Reread the pages where Clifford plays hide and seek with Emily Elizabeth. Talk about why Clifford did not choose a very good hiding place if he did not want to be found. Then, take children outside on the playground for a game. Designate a "home base." Have one child cover her eyes and count to 20 while the other children hide. (Hide with them for extra fun since children love it when their teachers join in games.)

When the child who is counting calls, "Ready or not, here I come!" the other children should try to tag home base without being caught. The first child caught is "it" and will be the next seeker; if no one is caught, then the last child to reach base is "it." (You may need a volunteer to watch home base to prevent arguments about who should be "it" next.)

Art Connections

Our Own Dog Show

Reread the last five pages of the book and then talk about dog shows. Ask how many children have attended a dog show or seen one on television. Next, give each child art supplies and ask them to draw the best dogs that they can. Explain that all of the "dogs" will be entered into the classroom dog show to try to win a prize. When children have finished their drawings, have them cut out their dogs. After children have left for the day, either attach the dogs to a bulletin board or laminate them and prop them up in the classroom.

Then, make one copy of the Dog Show Trophy Pattern (page 18) for each dog in the show. Write silly awards in the blank spaces on the trophies, such as "Most Spots" and "Friendliest Looking Dog." Award each dog a prize by placing the trophies next to the dogs. If time permits, have the award ceremony during class. Reward the "owners" by passing out dog-bone-shaped candy or Scooby-Doo™ cookies or crackers.

Creative Dramatics Connections

Our Own Clifford

In the dramatic play center of your classroom, create a scenario where children can play with Clifford and his tiny dog friends. On a table in the center, place a large, stuffed dog (red, if possible) and then add much smaller, plastic dogs. (Actual Clifford the Big Red Dog® character dolls are available at toy stores.) Also, add small people, a dollhouse, a box large enough for the stuffed dog, toy cars and trucks, and any other items that can contribute to the scene. Give each child time in the center to play with the giant dog and the tiny ones. If possible, provide additional Clifford books in this center and in the language arts center to further inspire children.

Dog Bone and Dog Show Trophy Patterns

Dog bone directions are found on page 16. Trophy directions are found on page 17.

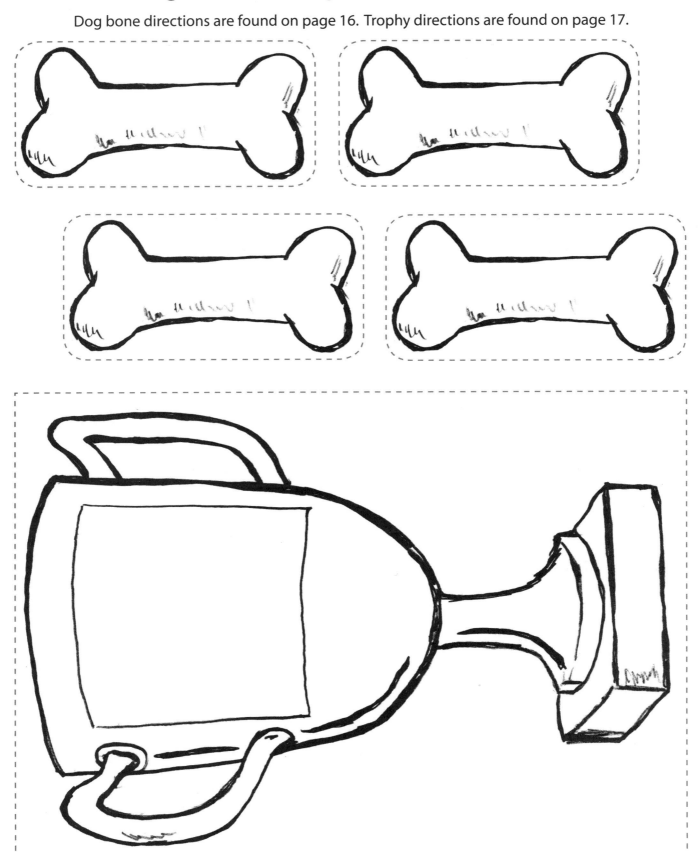

Matching Dogs

Directions: Oh no! The dogs in Clifford's neighborhood have escaped from their owners! Draw a line to match each dog with its owner. Hint: Look at the pictures the owners are holding for help.

CORDUROY

Written and illustrated by
by Don Freeman
Copyright 1968
Viking Books

Story Summary

Corduroy is a teddy bear who lives on a shelf in a department store. A little girl is shopping with her mother when she sees Corduroy and falls in love with him. The girl's mother does not want to buy Corduroy because he is missing a button and does not look new. Later that evening after the shoppers are gone, Corduroy searches everywhere in the store hoping to find his lost button. His adventurous night leads to a happy ending the next morning.

Themes:
- home and family
- self-esteem
- friendship

Skills:
- oral language
- money skills
- observation
- visual recall
- position words

Vocabulary:
Corduroy, department, escalator, flights, mattress, night watchman, overalls, palace, toppled

Related Books:
A Pocket for Corduroy by Don Freeman (Viking, 1978)

Corduroy Goes to School story by B.G. Hennessy; based on the character created by Don Freeman (Viking, 2002)

Before the Story
Show the cover of the book and tell children that the story is about a stuffed bear named Corduroy. Ask children to raise their hands if they have special stuffed animals. Ask each child, "What is your animal's name? Why is it special?" Then, look at the cover again and ask what Corduroy is missing. When children figure out that he is missing a button, ask them if that makes any difference in how special he is.

During the Story
Discuss the new vocabulary as you read the story. Let a child describe each word. Then, act out the words *escalator*, *toppled*, and *night watchman*.

After the Story
Let children use the Corduroy Puppets (patterns on page 23) to retell the story. Then, have children make up new stories about Corduroy and Lisa. Encourage them to refer back to the book to help them remember the story. If possible, provide other books in the Corduroy series for children to explore.

Language Arts Connections

What Happens at Night

Use the intrigue of a locked, dark, empty-of-shoppers store to spark class discussion and help children work on their oral language skills. Ask them what they think happens at night in a department store. Let children take turns telling about a nighttime adventure that might happen.

I Have Always Wanted . . .

Reread the parts in the book where Corduroy says what he "has always wanted": to climb a mountain, to live in a palace, to sleep in a bed, to have a home, and to have a friend. Ask children which of these things they think they want most and why. Let each child choose something he has always wanted and dictate or write a sentence about it starting with the words, "I have always wanted . . ." Then, let children draw pictures to illustrate their sentences. Allow time for children to show their pictures and read their sentences to the class.

Math Connections

Shopping

Children love the idea of having their own money to spend. Set up a shelf for toys labeled with price tags and provide play money. Let children take turns counting out the amount of money shown on each price tag.

Estimation

Give each child a small sheet of paper and let children estimate (guess) how much money the little girl paid to buy Corduroy. Collect the papers and make a bar graph with the results. Ask children to name the highest and lowest cost estimates, as well as the amount that had the most guesses.

Sorting Buttons

Provide a plastic jar of assorted buttons and several plastic bowls. Place these on a table or in the manipulative center. Include directions for sorting the buttons in different ways: color, size, shape, number of holes, etc. Tailor the directions to the buttons in your collection.

Science Connections

Textures

Help improve children's observation skills and their senses of touch using fabric. Place several different kinds of fabric into a shoe box. Make sure the fabrics have a variety of textures and colors and be sure to include a swatch of corduroy. Let each child take a few minutes to touch, look at, and even smell the swatches. Discuss which fabrics feel smooth, fuzzy, rough, scratchy, slippery, heavy, thin, and so on. Ask children to explain the differences between corduroy and the other fabrics.

Day and Night

Recall that Corduroy's story takes place both during the day and at night. Go outside. Ask children how they know whether it is day or night. Talk about things that typically happen in the daytime and at nighttime. Let children demonstrate their observations. Turn out the classroom lights and let them act out something that happens at night. Then, let them act out daytime events with the lights on.

Problem-Solving and Social Skills Connections

Memory Skills

The drawings in this book are perfect for helping children work on recall skills. Show a small group the first page for 10 seconds. Then, hide the page and ask children to recall what items were on the shelf (clown, rabbit, Corduroy, doll, and giraffe). Repeat for 20 seconds with the illustration of the furniture department and ask children to name the colors of the beds (blue, orange, white, and green) and what was on the tables (candles, flowers, lamps, and tablecloths). Finally, show the little girl's room for 20 seconds and then ask children to name everything they saw in the room.

Patience

Ask children if they know what it means to be patient. When you have a few responses, explain that Corduroy was very patient as he searched for his button. He looked carefully and did not get upset when he could not find it. Ask children to talk about times when they were patient.

Fine Motor Connections

My Own Corduroy

Let children make their own Corduroy bears. Give each child a copy of the Stuffed Corduroy pattern (page 24). Have each child color, cut out, and then trace around the bear on another piece of paper. Next, children should color and cut out their traced patterns. Help children staple the two bear patterns together, leaving the bottom of the feet open. Have children stuff their bears with cotton balls or shredded paper; then, tape the bears shut. Finally, let each child glue two buttons onto the stuffed bear's overall straps.

Let's Sew

Bring a large button, a needle, and thread to class. Demonstrate the basics of sewing a button onto fabric. (It does not have to be perfect for children to get the idea.) Then, give each child a lacing card, a lacing card string or shoelace, and a button with very large holes. (You can also make large buttons from heavy cardboard.) Let children "sew" the buttons to the lacing cards.

Gross Motor Connections

Obstacle Course

Use an obstacle course to help children learn position words from the story. Set up chairs, hoops, cones, tables, and other obstacles on the playground or in an open area. Next to each obstacle, place a card with a position word from the story. (For older children you may want to write specific directions instead of isolating each word.) Position words include *in*, *down*, *on*, *under*, *onto*, *up*, *off*, *around*, *over*, *above*, and *into*. You may want to pair the position words with opposite meanings to make them easier to remember.

Find the Missing Button

Keep working on position words by playing "Find the Missing Button!" Choose one child to cover her eyes while you hide a button in view of the other children. Then, let classmates direct the chosen child to find where the button is hidden.

Instruct classmates to only use position words, such as, "Look up!" and "Look under!" It may take some practice for children to avoid giving away the exact location too soon.

Art Connections

Decorate a Store

Sometimes, the way a store's merchandise is arranged is just as important as what is actually for sale. Talk with children about window-shopping and ask them to give examples of stores they want to go into because of the way things look in the window. Provide catalogs to give further examples of merchandising. Ask children to bring in toys they do not mind sharing and label the toys with their names. Empty a bookshelf and pile the toys in front of it. Let children take turns arranging the toys on the bookshelf so that a shopper would want to come in and buy the toys. If it is holiday time, let children add seasonal items, such as paper hearts, fall leaves and pumpkins, tinsel and ornaments, or gelt and unlit candles. After each child finishes their arrangement, let them decorate their own toy store sign with their name on it. Then, photograph them standing next to the arrangement of toys with the sign.

Creative Dramatics Connections

Let's Go Shopping

After children have arranged the toys in the Art Connections activity (left) get permission from parents and children to move the toys into the dramatic play area. Let children take turns being shoppers and clerks. Add a cash register, play money, shopping carts, and shopping bags. When you are ready for the toys to return to their owners, have a toy store "clearance" sale and let children take home their own items.

I Like You Just the Way You Are

Talk about the fact that Lisa wanted Corduroy even though he did not look new. Reread the sentence, "I like you the way you are" at the end of the story. Give children an opportunity to emulate Lisa's kindness. Have children sit in chairs in a circle. Choose a child to stand and tell her, "I like you the way you are because . . ." Have that child remain standing and tell the classmate on her right something she likes about him. They remain standing as he picks the next child. Continue the game around the circle until everyone is standing.

Corduroy Puppets

Directions: Copy, color, and cut out these puppets. Then, laminate and glue them to craft sticks. Let children use the puppets to retell the story of Corduroy.

Stuffed Corduroy

Directions: Lisa wanted Corduroy for her very own bear. You can make your own stuffed bear. Color this bear, cut it out, and your teacher will tell you how to finish it.

Curious George

Written and illustrated by
by H. A. Rey and Margret Rey
Copyright 1978, Houghton Mifflin

Story Summary

George is a curious monkey who lives in Africa. He is captured by a man in a big yellow hat who takes George home to live in the zoo. George's curiosity leads him into several adventures, such as accidentally calling the fire department and floating away with a bunch of balloons. Although George is not always happy, children enjoy his childlike wonder at his new surroundings.

Themes:
- animals
- curiosity
- emotions
- travel

Skills:
- text cues
- number words
- money
- physics
- emotions
- balance

Vocabulary:
Africa, curious, gusts, lifebelt, naughty, overboard, signal, watchman

Related Books:
Curious George Flies a Kite
by H. A. Rey and Margret Rey
(Houghton Mifflin, 1977)

Curious George Gets a Medal
by H. A. Rey and Margret Rey
(Houghton Mifflin, 1957)

Before the Story

Ask children what it would be like to have a pet that was very smart and very, very curious. Explain that Curious George is a monkey that comes from far away. Show children the continent of Africa on a world map or a globe; then, trace your finger to New York and continue on to your state so that children can get an idea of the story's setting.

Loud Words

"Finally he HAD to try."

"WHERE IS GEORGE?"

"DING-A-LING-A-LING! GEORGE HAD TELEPHONED THE FIRE STATION!"

"HURRAY! HURRAY! HURRAY!"

During the Story

Help children with the vocabulary of the story. Also, point out the many places in the story where the text is written in all uppercase letters. Explain that these words should be said more loudly than the other words.

After the Story

Ask children, since George got into so much trouble, whether they think the zoo is a better place for him than the home of the man with the big yellow hat. Talk about the differences between living at the zoo and living in a house. Where is George likely to be safer? Where is he more likely to do silly things?

Language Arts Connections

Visual Clues

Learning to recognize visual cues within the text is very important. Show children the portions of text written in all uppercase letters. Ask children to repeat the sentences after you with appropriate emphasis and volume. In each instance, ask children why they think the words are very important. For example, on page 20, the words "WHERE IS GEORGE?" are uppercase because George is missing. The sailors know that on a ship, a missing person can mean something dangerous has happened; in fact, George has fallen overboard! Let children read and chant all of the uppercase words as you reread the entire book together.

Math Connections

Number Fun

For younger children, review page 30 in the book where George dials the telephone. Write the number words on the board. Let children take turns coming to the board to write the numerals that match the number words. If possible, supply an old rotary dial telephone. Give children different number sequences and have them practice recognizing the numbers and dialing them.

Balloon Man

Older children will love playing "balloon man." Purchase a bunch of helium balloons. Tie a weight to each balloon. Set up a cash register nearby with toy money or real coins. Write prices for the balloons on poster board and post it next to the balloons. For example, you could charge 25¢ for a yellow balloon, 50¢ for a red balloon, and $1.00 for a green balloon. Give each child some money and let them choose balloons to "buy." Help each child count out the correct amount of change. Then, use the balloons for the Science Connections activity (below left).

Science Connections

Lighter Than Air

Use the balloons from the Math Connections activity (above right) to talk about science. Explain that helium, the gas inside the balloons, is lighter than air. Helium makes the balloons so light they can float off the ground. Provide several small objects such as blocks, toy cars, plastic links, plastic spoons, and small dolls. Help children place each object on a postal scale and record its name and weight on a graph. Then, tie each object to a single balloon's string. Observe if the object floats or sinks and record on the graph whether the balloon could lift each object off the ground.

If children are particularly interested, expand the experiment by tying two balloons to each object. If children are old enough, distribute the balloons at the end of class.

Caution: Before completing any balloon activity, ask families about possible latex allergies. Also, remember that uninflated or popped balloons may present a choking hazard.

Problem-Solving and Social Skills Connections

Emotions

Poor George experiences a lot of ups and downs in this book. Children may be concerned about his worry during some of his adventures, even though George looks very happy in most illustrations. As you reread the book, talk about each of the feelings and emotions George has: curious, sad, tired, fascinated, frightened, and probably happy at the end of the story. Give each child a small hand mirror or gather a small group together in front of a larger mirror. Tell children to make the faces they would expect George to have in each part of the story. For example, say, "George is curious. How does your face look when you feel curious?"

After each child has had a turn at the mirror, let them draw pictures of themselves feeling one of the emotions. If time permits, ask children to write or dictate about a time they felt that way and record it on the back of their papers.

Fine Motor Connections

Yummy Bananas

Most children like bananas, so use George as inspiration for them to learn to help themselves. Ask parents to send in unpeeled bananas. Talk about how George eats bananas in the jungle. Give one to each child and tell them to push their fingernails into the top of the bananas just under the stem. (This creates a weak spot so that the peel will separate easily.) Then, demonstrate how to pull back the banana's stem and open the peel to expose the banana underneath.

If children are old enough, let them eat the bananas for a snack. For younger children, gather the peeled bananas and cut them into circles. Then, toss the banana slices together with pineapple and mango chunks for a tropical fruit salad snack.

George's New Home Maze

Copy George's New Home maze (page 29) for each child. Tell children to draw a line to help the monkey get to the zoo.

Gross Motor Connections

Balance

Turn to page 42 in the book where George is walking across the telephone lines. Show the picture and then ask children what they need to be able to do in order to walk across something as thin as a wire. Explain the meaning of the word *balance*. To demonstrate the skill of balancing, have children try to stand on one foot. Encourage them to stretch out their arms to help them stay upright. Then, take the class outside. On level, grassy ground, place two long jump ropes in parallel lines, about one and a half feet apart. Let children take turns trying to balance like George as they walk along the ropes with one foot on each. Give them hints like: Do not move too quickly. Turn your feet slightly outwards. Hold out your arms for extra balance, and so on.

Art Connections

Jungle Home

Talk about the word *home*. Ask, "Where is George's home? Do you think he misses his home?" Discuss the fact that, until the man in the yellow hat captures him, George's home is in the jungle. To imagine what it was like in George's home, create a jungle atmosphere. Let children help you attach tree trunks (long strips of brown paper) to the walls. Enlarge and copy the Leaf and Flower Patterns (page 28) and let children color and cut them out. You can also cut leaves from green garbage bags. Attach the leaves and flowers to the walls and the ceiling, if possible, and twist long strips of green or brown fabric to be vines. Add appropriate stuffed animals to the area, such as monkeys, tigers, snakes, bats, and birds. Play jungle music or nature sounds and let children enter the area for reading time. Children may also visit the jungle to act out the parts of the man in the yellow hat, George, or another creature who lives in the jungle.

Creative Dramatics Connections

Let's Be Animals

This book offers a great opportunity for a collaborative project in creative dramatics. Gather as many zoo animal costumes as you can. These do not have to be elaborate. Use simple masks, paint animal bodies on thrift store pillowcases and cut out arm and leg holes, or use face paint.

If possible, create different stations around the room in which children can dress up like some of the animals found on the last page of *Curious George* (zebra, giraffe, rhinoceros, camel, penguin, etc.). Make sure you have a monkey costume, as well. Assign one child to be George and let other children become the zoo animals. (If you are using face paint, ask for parent volunteers to help children prepare so that all of them will be ready at about the same time.) Then, let children pretend George has arrived at the zoo and the other animals are welcoming him to his new home.

Leaf and Flower Patterns

Directions are found on page 27.

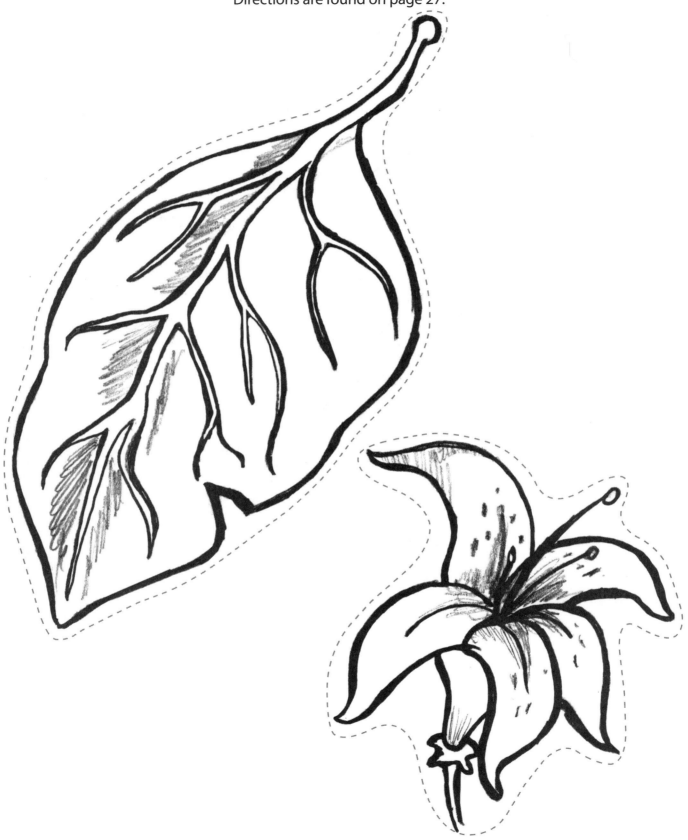

George's New Home

Directions: Help George find his way to his new home.
Draw a line from the monkey to the zoo.

DIARY OF A WORM

Written by Doreen Cronin
Illustrated by Harry Bliss
Copyright 2003
Joanna Cotler Books

Story Summary

This unusual book chronicles some interesting events that happen over several months in the life of an earthworm. The worm describes his attempts to walk upside down like his friend Spider, his need to plan ahead to avoid becoming bait during fishing season, and various school day anecdotes. Children will enjoy and remember the earthworm facts that are scattered though this humorous book.

Themes:
- science and nature
- self-awareness

Skills:
- journaling
- alike and different
- counting to 100
- home and family

Vocabulary:
breathe, diary, fishing, garbage, homework, manners, nightmare, swallowed, tomorrow, tunnels

Related Books:
Diary of a Spider
by Doreen Cronin
(Joanna Cotler, 2005)

Click Clack Moo: Cows That Type
by Doreen Cronin
(Simon & Schuster, 2000)

Before the Story

Ask children if they have ever kept a diary. Find out what kinds of information children expect to find in a diary. Can anyone keep a diary? Are there dates in the diary? What might they learn from reading a diary's entry? Then, introduce the book.

During the Story

Stop as you read the story and ask if the worm ever does anything that sounds like something they would do. For example, do they tease their brothers or sisters? Do their brothers or sisters tease them? Do they think about what they want to be when they grow up? Do they ever have disagreements with their friends? Most children will probably have at least one experience in common with the worm.

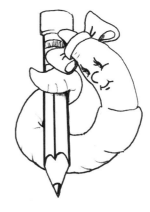

After the Story

Let each child name one reason he might like to be a worm and one reason he likes being a person. All in all, the worm in the story seems to like who he is. Encourage children who are comfortable doing so to share something they like about being themselves.

Language Arts Connections

Classroom Diary

Just like the worm keeps a diary, either let individual children keep diaries or, especially for prewriters, keep one as a class. Use copies of the Diary Page (page 33), a notebook, or chart paper. Each day or each week, set aside a few minutes to jot down notes about specific happenings. The notes can be about class or community events, but they can also be recordings of observations made by one or more of the children. Let children dictate the entries to you if they cannot write yet.

At a later date, show the value of keeping a diary by reading or letting children read some of the earlier entries aloud to the class. Then, talk about the fact that writing things down can help them remember what has happened and that it is fun to look back on previous events.

Math Connections

Count to 100

Turn to the page in the story where the first of 600 ants are shown in a line. Tell children they will practice learning to count to 600 as a class. Provide sets of manipulatives to represent the ants. If possible, use items mentioned or shown in the story, such as 100 plastic bugs (ants or spiders), 100 bottle tops, 100 macaroni noodles, 100 marbles, 100 pieces of gum, and 100 silk leaves. (You can also use torn bits of sponge, which will look like the ants' food.)

Keep each set in its own bin for children to practice counting. Each time a child is successful, add a new set. For example, when a child can count 100 ants, add 100 bottle tops. When all children have reached the goal, line up all 600 manipulatives around the room like a trail of ants. At the end of the trail, make a small mound of packaged sweet treats. Cover it with a plastic bowl to represent an anthill. As each children reach the end, reward them by letting them choose treats from the anthill.

Science Connections

Real Worms

Children will be eager to observe real worms. Dig up worms or purchase some from a bait shop. House them in an aquarium and help children research worm care. The soil should contain manure and be at least 8" (20 cm) deep. It can also contain other materials like peat moss, straw, or cardboard. Gently water the soil periodically and add fruit and vegetable scraps, coffee grounds, and eggshells (no animal products) to provide food for the earthworms. Bury the food a few inches deep to keep other pests like fruit flies away.

Let children observe the worms for several weeks and have them record their observations on the Field Notes Template (page 34). Children should take notes about what happens to the food, the weights and lengths of the worms, and soil conditions. Eventually, dig a hole outside and set the worms free. Do not release the worms if it is too cold for them to safely burrow underground.

Problem-Solving and Social Skills Connections

Venn Diagram

Worm's friend Spider makes several appearances throughout the story, although the two seem like an unlikely pair. Draw a Venn diagram on the board and ask children to name things that are alike and different about the friends. For example, Worm has no legs and cannot walk upside down like Spider, and Spider cannot dig in dirt. But, Worm and Spider laugh at the same things and enjoy spending time together.

Then, help each child make a Venn diagram about what is alike and different about a good friend and themselves. Help them think of similarities and differences that they like. For example, they may like that they both live in the same neighborhood. They may also like that their friend has a big brother who is nice to both of them. Explain that having things in common makes it easy to enjoy our friends, and having differences makes the friendships interesting.

Fine Motor Connections

Macaroni Necklaces

Turn to the page where the worm children make macaroni necklaces. Talk about why they only used one noodle each. (Where would a string necklace "rest" since the worms have no shoulders?) Then, make macaroni necklaces as a class. Provide string precut into approximately 24" (61 cm) lengths and dry macaroni noodles. If desired, let children color their noodles with markers before threading them onto the string. Then, tie the necklaces loosely around children's necks. (For very young children, do not make necklaces since this can be a choking hazard. Instead, just complete the stringing portion of the activity.) As a treat afterward, enjoy eating macaroni like the worms did. Make some macaroni and cheese and share it as a snack.

Caution: Before completing any food activity, ask families' permission and inquire about students' food allergies and religious or other food preferences.

Gross Motor Connections

Hokey Pokey

Share the page where the worm children do the hokey pokey. Then, have children do the dance "worm style," meaning that they can only stick their heads in and out. Ask them how they can do the dance differently since they are humans. Then, either sing the whole song or play a recorded version and do the hokey pokey together like humans (using arms, feet, shoulders, elbows, and knees instead of just heads). When the song is over, let children take turns suggesting silly body parts to do the hokey pokey with, such as bellies or eyelashes or teeth.

Art Connections

Make a Stuffed Worm

Make an art project children will love to play with. Ask parents for donations of old pairs of panty hose. Wash the hose and hang them to dry; then, cut off the legs. Provide cotton batting and let each child select a leg and stuff it with the batting to create their own worm. After each worm is stuffed, knot the open end to keep the stuffing in and the hose from unraveling. Then, provide glue, fabric scraps, felt pieces, yarn, buttons, and even doll accessories, such as jewelry or hats with elastic straps, and invite each child to personalize his worm. If you have enough supplies, you can also cut off the feet of additional pairs of hose. Have children stuff the feet of the hose; then, knot them, cut off the excess, and add legs made of yarn or rope to create spider friends.

Creative Dramatics Connections

Worm Tunnels

As you observe the worms from the Science Connections activity (page 31), talk with children about how the worms move around. Ask why Worm cannot do things like dance the hokey pokey with very many body parts, why he can fit inside a piece of macaroni, and why he is good at tunneling through the dirt. Explain that earthworms move by pushing tiny bristles into the ground and then expanding and contracting their muscles to pull themselves along. Create an earthworm experience in your classroom. Open the ends of large cardboard boxes to create tunnels or hang sheets over low clotheslines and anchor the edges of the sheets apart on the floor. Let children pretend to be earthworms tunneling through the earth. Not only is this good exercise, they will soon realize that squirming along on the ground is much more difficult than it looks!

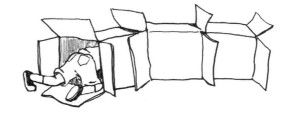

Diary Page

_____

_____

_____

_____

_____

_____

_____

_____

Name _____

Field Notes Template

Draw what you see in the earthworm box.

Date: _____

Notes: _____

_____

_____

Draw what you see in the earthworm box.

Date: _____

Notes: _____

_____

_____

Draw what you see in the earthworm box.

Date: _____

Notes: _____

_____

_____

Draw what you see in the earthworm box.

Date: _____

Notes: _____

_____

_____

GOODNIGHT MOON

Written by Margaret Wise Brown
Illustrated by Clement Hurd
Copyright 1975
HarperTrophy

Story Summary

The little bunny in the nursery knows that it is time for bed. However, he has another agenda. In this gentle, rhythmic story, the bunny stalls and stalls as he says good night to everything in his room. More than an hour after he begins, he finally drops off to sleep.

Themes:
- home and family
- scheduling and time
- light and dark

Skills:
- rhyming words
- telling time
- sequencing
- knitting
- visual discrimination

Vocabulary:
everywhere, goodnight, great, mush, nobody, toyhouse

Related Books:
Good Night, Gorilla
by Peggy Rathmann
(Putnam, 1996)

My World
by Margaret Wise Brown
(HarperCollins, 2001)

Before the Story

Ask children what their favorite bedtime stories are. Explain that you are going to read a favorite bedtime story about a little bunny who is going to bed. Then, ask who or what children say good night to each night. Children will notice during the reading that this bunny says good night to everything in sight! Also, note that two of the words in the story, *goodnight* and *toyhouse*, are each usually spelled as two separate words.

During the Story

Point out that there are different kinds of pictures in this book. Some are in color and some are black and white. The color illustrations show scenes of the entire room, while the black and white illustrations focus on details from the larger pictures.

After the Story

Turn to one of the pages that shows the entire room and ask children to name the things in the bunny's room that are the same as things in their own rooms. Let each child choose something in the picture they would also like to have in their own rooms.

Language Arts Connections

Rhyming Words

This book is basically an illustrated poem. Children will be able to join in to complete the sentences with you if you supply the first rhyming word. Facilitate the association of rhyming words by saying each word in isolation to see if children can name its rhyme or rhymes. The rhymes are: *balloon/moon, bears/chairs, kittens/mittens, toyhouse/mouse/house, brush/mush/hush, clocks/socks,* and *air/everywhere.* Continue by letting children come up with more rhyming pairs to wish "Goodnight." Give an example, such as, "Goodnight frog, goodnight dog." Then, let children add their own rhymes.

Learn Some Rhymes

Teach children "Hey, Diddle, Diddle" and "Three Little Kittens" since the cow jumping over the moon and kittens are featured in the story. Help children compare the words in the nursery rhymes to those in *Goodnight Moon.* Make a Venn diagram to show which rhyming pairs appear in more than one nursery rhyme and/or book.

Math Connections

Telling Time

Look at the picture with the words "Goodnight clocks/And goodnight socks." Talk about what time it is on both clocks. (The clocks on this page show 7:40.) Turn to some of the other pages and look at the times. Note that at the very beginning of the story, the time is 7:00, but, by the end of the story, it is 8:10. Do the following activity to see whether children can figure out how much time passes from the beginning of the book to the end (1 hour and 10 minutes). Provide several small teaching clocks for groups of two or three. Start at the beginning of the book and say, "It is 7:00. Everyone turn their clocks' hands to show 7:00."

Check children's clocks, correct any mistakes, and then turn to the next picture that has clocks. Say, "It is now 10 minutes after 7:00. Turn your clocks' hands to show 10 minutes after 7:00." Repeat with all of the pages in the book that show clocks. Finally, discuss with children the total amount of time that passes in the book.

Science Connections

Getting Darker

Show the color pictures of the bunny's room again. Point out that each picture is a little darker than the last. It becomes harder and harder to see small details, and the colors are not as vivid. Explain that people need light in order to see color. Do an experiment to demonstrate this phenomenon. Place two balloons in a box: one red and one blue. Cover the opening of the box with a large, heavy, black cloth or a few large towels. Test the activity by closing your eyes and putting your head under the cloth. You should not be able to see the colors of the balloons, but you should still be able to make out two balloon shapes. Let the children close their eyes, put their head under the cloth, look at the balloons, and try to guess what colors they are. Record the children's guesses; then, remove the balloons so that children can see if they were correct.

Caution: Before completing any balloon activity, ask families about possible latex allergies. Also, remember that uninflated or popped balloons may present a choking hazard.

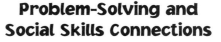

Problem-Solving and Social Skills Connections

Bedtime

Many, many children fight going to bed. Just like the bunny in this story, they think of all kinds of ways to stall the inevitable time to sleep. Talk with children about your bedtime routine and explain what you do each night to get ready for bed. (Since children often cannot imagine their teacher outside of school, they will be very interested to hear what you really do!) Ask children to talk about whether they like to go to bed and why or why not. Then, use the Sequencing Cards (page 38) to help children talk about what they do before bedtime. The cards show a bunny reading some books, having a snack, brushing his teeth, and putting on pajamas and saying good night to his room. Color, cut out, and laminate the cards. Then, let children work in small groups and take turns putting the cards in order. Children can eliminate cards for activities they do not do before bed or draw new ones to show additional activities.

Fine Motor Connections

Knitting

In the book, the old lady whispering "hush" spends her time rocking and knitting. If children are old enough, provide balls of yarn, children's knitting needles, and crochet hooks and allow children to pretend to knit or crochet. If you or a classroom parent knows how to knit, spend time with a few children each day teaching them how to cast on stitches. You may even demonstrate how to knit or purl a few stitches for interested children to try to copy. After the knitting sessions, have children wind the yarn into balls for next time.

Bunny's Rug

Let children use variegated yarn to make rugs like the one on the floor of the bunny's room. Point out a picture of the rug as an example. Give each child a sheet of heavy paper and help them smear glue on it. Then, demonstrate how to wind the yarn in a spiral on the glue. Have children start in the center of the paper and make increasingly larger circles. When the glue is dry, cut off the excess paper, leaving only the yarn "rug."

Visual Discrimination Connections

Where Is the Mouse?

Clement Hurd, the illustrator, has provided in each full color picture a tiny mouse character that moves around and can be difficult to find. Spend a little time with each child to help them find the mouse in each picture, point to where it is, and name the activity it is doing. After each child has had a turn, try to find a big book version of the story. Let children call out when they see the mouse as you turn the pages. After a child calls out the location of the mouse, let him choose another child to tell what the mouse is doing. After a pair of children have found the mouse, they must remain quiet during subsequent turns so that everyone gets a chance to "shout out the mouse." Give children additional practice by letting them find and circle all of the hidden mice on the Where Are the Mice? reproducible (page 39).

Art Connections

Artwork for My Room

Point out the beautiful artwork in the bunny's room. One picture is of the nursery rhyme "Hey, Diddle, Diddle" and the other is probably a picture from the fairy tale "Goldilocks and the Three Bears."

Have children make artwork for their own "nurseries." First, children will make frames that will fit over a piece of 8½" x 11" (21.6 cm x 27.9 cm) paper. Let children cut out the centers of sturdy paper to make the frames and then decorate them with gold crayon and glitter. While the frames dry, let each child browse through books of nursery rhymes and fairy tales and choose a scene they would like to draw. Help children sketch their drawings in pencil and then complete them with paint, crayons, or colorful pencils.

Place the frames on the completed paintings and tape or glue them together. Protect each framed picture by placing it between two sheets of waxed paper or cardboard, stapled together, and send the pictures home to be displayed in each child's room.

Creative Dramatics Connections

Time to Sleep

Sleepy time can be fun time, too. In a corner of your room, prepare a sleeping bag, blankets, and pillows. Provide *Goodnight Moon* and some other sleepy time favorites. Let children take turns pretending to go to bed. They can go quietly or they can try to find ways to stall, like the bunny did in the story. Take a turn with each child by letting them tell you something to which they would like to say "good night" before they pretend to drop off to sleep.

Extend the scenario above by putting children in their parents'"slippers." Let children play in pairs. Assign one child to be the nanny and the other to be the child going to bed. Let the nanny pretend to try to get the child to go to sleep, while the child tries to find ways to stay up later.

Sequencing Cards
Directions are found on page 36.

Where Are the Mice?

Directions: Find the hiding mice and circle them.

HAROLD and the PURPLE CRAYON

Written and illustrated
by Crockett Johnson
Copyright 1983, HarperCollins

Story Summary

Harold is quite an artist! Instead of going to bed, he decides to go for a walk in the moonlight and he takes his purple crayon along. He draws the moon—and the sidewalk and a tree and a balloon and a big adventure for himself. He draws his way into and out of several difficult situations, but he ends up safe and happy in his very own bed—also drawn with purple crayon.

Themes:
- imagination
- resourcefulness
- exploration
- colors

Skills:
- predicting
- phonemic awareness
- fractions
- drawing conclusions
- prewriting
- safety

Vocabulary:
ashore, deserving, farther, frightening, moonlight, realized, terribly, wondering

Related Books:
Harold's Fairy Tale
by Crockett Johnson
(HarperTrophy, 1994)

Harold at the North Pole
by Crockett Johnson
(HarperTrophy, 2004)

Before the Story

Practice the comprehension skill of predicting with this book. Show children the book's cover and ask what they think Harold is going to draw with his purple crayon. Record their guesses. Then, as you read the story to discover what Harold actually does draw, you can place a check mark by each item or scene on the list that the children guessed correctly.

1. house
2. cat
3. dog
4. baby
5. boat ✔
6. car
7. book
8. train

During the Story

Continue to practice the skill of predicting. Harold gets into some precarious situations during the story. Pause before he solves each problem and ask children what they think Harold will do to get out of each situation. For example, when Harold accidentally draws himself into an ocean, ask children what Harold might do to get himself out of the ocean.

After the Story

This story has an ending that is somewhat ambiguous since Harold ends up in bed, but it is still a bed that he drew. Ask children to draw some conclusions about what they think really happened when Harold had his adventure. Is his bed really drawn with purple crayon? Is he really in his room at the end of the story? Are his walls covered with drawings in purple crayon? Was it all a dream, or did he have a real adventure?

Language Arts Connections

Phonemic Awareness

There are many words in this story that are fun to rhyme. Below is a list of suggested rhyming words. Have children listen to the words. Then, ask children if they can think of any other words that rhyme.

Next, say two words and ask children if the words rhyme. Repeat, making sure to vary the sets of words so that some word pairs rhyme and other word pairs do not rhyme.

Finally, say sets of three words, making sure that two of the words rhyme and one word does not rhyme. Ask children to identify the two rhyming words or, alternatively, ask them to identify the word in the set that does not rhyme.

Rhyming word suggestions:
- cake, rake, snake, lake, wake, fake,
- play, day, way, stay, fray, lay, may, hay, away
- toy, boy, joy, Troy
- boat, gloat, moat, float, bloat
- draw, straw, law, paw, caw

Math Connections

Harold Likes to Measure

Provide children with the opportunity to learn how to use a small ruler. Give each child a copy of "Harold Likes to Measure" (page 43). The children should cut out the ruler at the bottom of the page. Next, they should hold the ruler under each line to measure the length. Circle the correct answer next to each line.

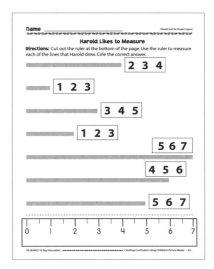

Science Connections

Sink and Float

Harold sinks in the water he draws, but the boat he draws floats—why? Explore the concepts of weight and surface area with children. Explain that if weight is spread over a larger space on the water, it will float. This is why a small pebble sinks, but a huge, heavy boat with a big, flat bottom will float. Fill a tub with water and give each child a piece of clay. Have each child roll the clay into a ball and take turns dropping it into the water. The clay balls should sink. Then, have each child retrieve his clay and form it into a shape he thinks will float.

If you have some very small people figures, let children try to float them on their boats. (Before trying this activity with the figures, make sure the figures will sink but that they are not too heavy to float on top of the clay boats.)

Problem-Solving and Social Skills Connections

Harold Is a Great Problem Solver!

Harold is actually quite a resourceful character who solves many problems. For example, he draws his own shortcut, creates a dragon to guard his apple tree, makes a boat to save himself in the ocean, draws a picnic when he is hungry, creates animal friends to finish the leftover pie from the picnic, makes a hot air balloon to save himself from falling, and, when he finally remembers how to find his window, draws it and his bed. Reread the book to children and point out all of the pages where Harold solves problems.

As a class, choose one or two of the problems, such as Harold needing to find a guardian for the apple tree or falling off the mountain into thin air. Brainstorm other ways to solve the problems. Let each child draw a new solution to one of Harold's problems—using a purple crayon, of course.

Fine Motor Connections

Draw like Harold Draws

Harold spends a lot of time drawing lines. This is excellent fine motor and prewriting practice. Give each child a purple crayon and a copy of the Draw like Harold Draws reproducible (page 44). Children will draw the following lines and shapes:

1. long, straight line
2. jagged line like dragon teeth
3. wavy line like the ocean
4. triangle like the shape of a sail
5. circle like the shape of a round balloon
6. rectangle like the shape of buildings and windows

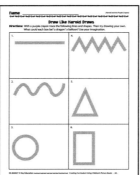

As children draw, ask them to imagine what each line might be. Can they see a dragon? A balloon? After each child is finished, you may choose to use the pages to assess each child's fine motor, drawing/prewriting, listening, and following directions skills.

Gross Motor Connections

High and Low

Children may not understand how visual perspective can change. For example, when Harold climbs to the top of the hill he draws, he is able to look around and see where he is. Demonstrate this concept with children while walking and developing gross motor skills. Take them outside and stand at a low point on the ground. Look around and talk about what you can see. Record your observations by taking pictures or video, if possible. Then, climb some hills or some stairs, just like Harold, and look back over the area where you were as well as around at the new scenery. Take more pictures or video and talk with children about what they are seeing, how it is different from the previous view, and whether they can see more from a higher point. Once you are back inside the classroom, compare the scenes on the video or the pictures and point out the differences.

Art Connections

Draw on Huge Paper

One of the most appealing things about Harold is his freedom to draw anywhere he wants. Try to give children some of the same freedom. Cover a large area, such as the walls in the hallway, with butcher paper. Give children purple crayons and let them cover the paper with art. If you cannot provide a large enough area to let each child have a fairly large space on which to work, allow a few children at a time to draw. Then, supply a new piece of paper for each group.

Scary Creatures

Children may be fascinated and a little concerned that Harold was able to draw something, such as the dragon, that actually scared him. Give children paper and crayons and ask them to draw an apple tree and then draw something they think would be a good creature to guard it. Let children share some tasty, red apple slices while they are drawing.

Creative Dramatics Connections

Are You Lost?

Most children fear getting lost. Even though Harold does the right thing by asking a policeman for help when he is lost, the policeman does not appear to be very helpful. Explain that police officers are usually very helpful, and children should never hesitate to tell a police officer if they are lost. Provide a police hat, badge, and navy blue shirt for children to use to role-play. Let one child at a time act as the police officer while other children take turns pretending they are lost and asking for help.

Bring in a large, cardboard appliance box and let children decorate it to look like a police station. Continue the role-play with "parents" coming to the police station to pick up their lost "children."

Harold Likes to Measure

Directions: Cut out the ruler at the bottom of the page. Use the ruler to measure each of the lines that Harold drew. Circle the correct answer.

2 3 (4)

1 2 3

3 4 5

1 2 3

5 6 7

4 5 6

5 6 7

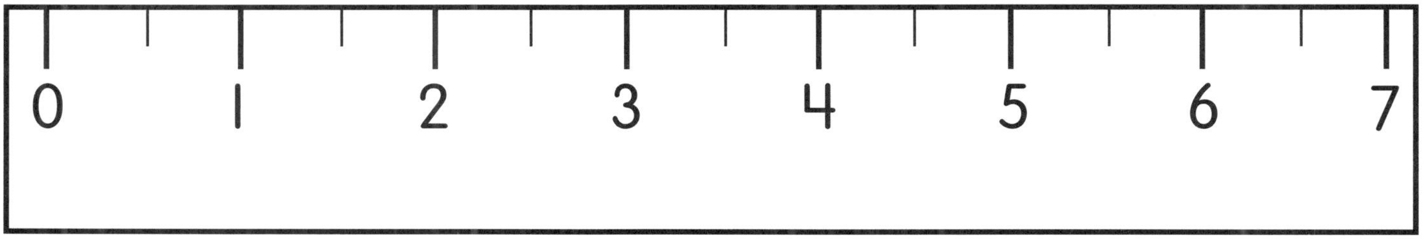

0 1 2 3 4 5 6 7

Draw like Harold Draws

Directions: Use a purple crayon to trace the lines and shapes. Then, draw your own.

1.

2.

3.

4.

5.

6.

IF YOU GIVE A MOUSE A COOKIE

Written by Laura Joffe Numeroff
Illustrated by Felicia Bond
Copyright 1985; Harper & Row, Publishers

Story Summary

Parents and teachers will find this circular tale familiar, since the mouse acts just like an energetic young child moving from activity to activity without missing a beat. The mouse eats a cookie, gives his hair a trim, sweeps the floor, draws a picture, and so on, until he eventually ends up back where he started—asking for a cookie again.

Themes:

- being a good host
- patience
- real and fantasy

Skills:

- making predictions
- alphabet
- counting
- biology
- manners

Vocabulary:

carried away, comfortable, finished, mustache, remind

Related Books:

If You Take a Mouse to School
by Laura Numeroff
(Laura Geringer, 2002)

If You Give a Moose a Muffin
by Laura Numeroff
(Laura Geringer, 1991)

Before the Story

Ask children what they think will happen if they give a mouse a cookie. Will he want more? Ask for a drink? Say, "Thank you"? Ask children what they do when they get a cookie.

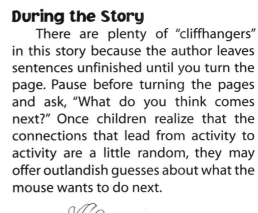

During the Story

There are plenty of "cliffhangers" in this story because the author leaves sentences unfinished until you turn the page. Pause before turning the pages and ask, "What do you think comes next?" Once children realize that the connections that lead from activity to activity are a little random, they may offer outlandish guesses about what the mouse wants to do next.

After the Story

This is a great story for multiple rereadings because children love to shout out what comes next. Let children retell the story as you turn the pages and show the pictures.

Language Arts Connections

Play with Letters

The cover of the book shows cookies drawn with crayons as if they were baking on a cookie sheet, and the title appears to be written in red crayon on the sheet. Instead of letting children write on a cookie sheet, give them another way to experiment with letters. Let children play with a set of magnetic letters and a cookie sheet. Challenge them to use the letters to spell out their names.

Alphabet Cookies

Purchase a set of alphabet cookie cutters (available at craft stores) and prepared sugar cookie dough. Give each child a small portion of dough and help them roll it out between two sheets of waxed paper. Either let each child make the first letter in their name or assign each child a few letters to make a cookie alphabet as a class. If you can, cut out and bake several cookie alphabets; then, have children practice spelling words from the story. You may also want to use cookies to spell out the title of the story, let children decorate the cookie letters with icing and sprinkles, and then eat the title.

Math Connections

Count with Cookies!

Give each child a copy of the Counting Chocolate Chips reproducible (page 48) and have them match each cookie to another with the same number of chips. To create a file folder game, enlarge the reproducible on sturdy paper, color the cookies light brown, cut them out, and laminate them. Draw a mouse in overalls on the cover of a file folder and write, "Can you help the mouse match the cookies with the same number of chips?" Staple a length of yarn to half of the cookies (make sure none of these have the same number of chips) and glue them to the left inside panel of the file folder. Glue magnets to the backs of the remaining cookies; then, glue these cookies to the right inside panel of the folder. Finally, measure the yarn from each cookie to its match, tie a paper clip to the yarn, and cut off the excess. Children can stretch each paper clip from the cookie on one side of the folder to the other to match the cookies with the same number of chips.

Science Connections

What Do Mice Really Eat?

In the story, the cookie given to the mouse appears to be chocolate chip. But, is that really the kind of food a mouse would prefer? If you have a fellow teacher or friend who keeps mice, set up an experiment to find out what foods a mouse might enjoy most. Gather food recommended for pet mice, such as vegetables, fruit, and rodent chow. (Do not give mice processed people food, uncooked beans or rice, animal products, cabbage, onion, hot peppers, or anything with sugar.) Place all of the food within a mouse's reach by spreading it out on a plate.

Let children guess which food they think the mouse will try first, will eat most often, and will finish first. Then, place the plate in the mouse's cage. Record the results. If possible, try the experiment a few more times, keeping the same food options but rearranging them on the plate. Then, graph the results of the experiment.

Problem-Solving and Social Skills Connections

Entertaining Guests

Ask children to recall how hard the boy works to keep his mouse friend happy. He offers the mouse refreshments, entertains him, makes a place for him to nap, and entertains and feeds him again. Ask children to think about when they have visited their friends or family. What did their friends do to make them feel comfortable when they were guests?

In your dramatic play center, spend a little one-on-one time pretending to be a guest in each child's home. Make a mouse puppet from a paper bag or use a stuffed mouse. Knock on a "door" and see what each child does to make the mouse feel welcome. Jot notes about each "visit." At the end of the week, acknowledge each child's hospitality by writing a thank-you note from the mouse. Sample notes could say: "Dear Josh, Thank you for offering me a glass of milk when I visited. Love, Mouse." or "Dear Darby, Thank you for the lovely talk during our visit. I had a good time. Sincerely, Mouse."

"Dear Josh, Thank you for offering me a glass of milk when I visited. Love, Mouse."

Fine Motor Connections

Refrigerator Art

Although art projects are usually reserved for the art center, they also provide fine motor skill practice. Reread the section of the book where the mouse draws a picture with crayons, signs his name, and then tapes the picture to the refrigerator. Give each child crayons and paper and ask them to draw pictures of a scene from the book or of their family like the mouse does. Carefully sign each child's name in script on a separate piece of paper and give it to them, along with a piece of tracing paper. Let the children use dark crayons to trace their names on the tracing paper. Tape the tracing paper to the artwork to show their signed name. Then, let each child attempt to tear off two pieces of tape and tape their picture to a door, wall, or bulletin board. (This can be tricky and is high-level fine motor practice. You may want to use masking tape instead of clear tape since masking tape can be gently pulled away from paper without damaging the artwork.)

Gross Motor Connections

Mouse-Inspired Cleaning

Sweeping and mopping strengthen large muscle groups and improve eye-hand coordination. Use props in your housekeeping center for a little mouse-inspired cleaning. Provide as many brooms and dustpans as possible and let children sweep the "hair" from the Art Connections activity (below, left) and place it in the trash. Play soft, slow music as children do this activity.

Remind children that the mouse got carried away and swept the entire house. Play some lively music and let children pretend to get carried away and sweep the entire classroom. If you are brave, provide small mops and slightly soapy water and let small groups take turns washing a section of the floor.

Art Connections

Barbershop Portraits

Children are often tempted to cut their own hair like the mouse does in the story. Give this desire an outlet by making barbershop portraits. Reread the book, paying special attention to the pages on which the mouse trims his hair. Help children use paint or crayons to draw large self-portraits on sheets of card stock. Then, let children use white glue and long scraps of yarn to add hair to their portraits. Have children smear plenty of glue where they wish to attach hair. Also, make sure they attach only one end of the pieces of yarn to the portraits.

After class, let the portraits dry and set up a barbershop, complete with safety scissors. Cover a low bulletin board in red and white strips of paper and use pushpins to attach some of the portraits to it. Let children whose portraits are posted cut the hair on their own portraits. When they are finished, post a second row of portraits. Display the new haircuts on the bulletin board.

For a quick and fun cleanup, proceed to the Gross Motor Connections activity (above, right).

Creative Dramatics Connections

Good Manners

Inspire good manners with dramatic play. Reread the section of the book where the mouse asks for a straw and a napkin with his cookie snack. Give children paper plates, empty cups and straws, and napkins.

Sit with children and pretend to be a group of mice. Pretend to drink milk and eat cookies. Demonstrate the proper way to eat a cookie over your plate, use your napkin, and drink carefully through a straw. Reward children's efforts with the real thing. Pass out a cookie for each child, and add a small amount of milk to each cup, and encourage children to use the good manners they have just learned. After the real food is eaten, have one child carry the wastebasket around to each child. Instruct children to carefully throw away their trash.

Counting Chocolate Chips

Directions: Draw lines to match the cookies that have the same number of chips.

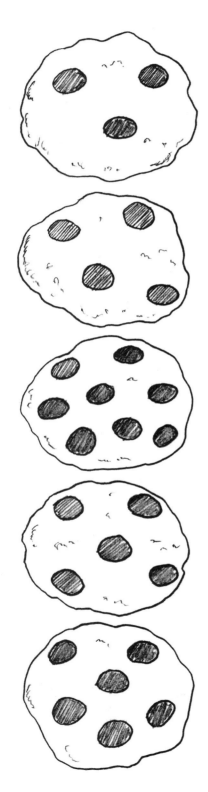
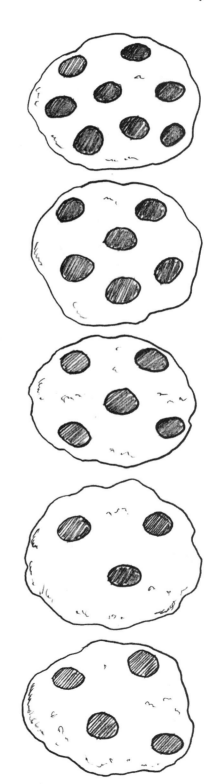

Take Care of Me!

Directions: The boy in the story worked hard to take care of the mouse. Color the pictures that show how someone in your family takes care of you.

Kitten's First Full Moon

Written and illustrated
by Kevin Henkes
Copyright 2004, Greenwillow Books

Story Summary

Poor Kitten! She sees a full moon for the first time and mistakes it for a very delicious bowl of milk. She tries her best to get to the bowl, but alas, it remains out of reach. After many unsuccessful attempts, Kitten gives up and goes home, only to find her loving owners have left her a delicious bowl of milk of her very own. Lucky Kitten!

Themes:
- perseverance
- space
- pets

Skills:
- fluency
- vowel sounds
- calendar math
- setting goals

Vocabulary:
edge, lucky, raced, thought, tongue, tumbled, waiting, wiggled

Related Books:
Owen
by Kevin Henkes
(Greenwillow, 1993)

Papa, Please Get the Moon for Me
by Eric Carle
(Little Simon, 1999)

Before the Story

Ask who has seen the full moon. Show the full moon on the book's cover. Help children make a list of the different things they think a full moon looks like. If children need prompting, suggest a marshmallow, a water chestnut, a volleyball, or a golf ball.

During the Story

As you read the story, each time Kitten tries a new way of getting the moon, ask children what they think is going to happen to her. Will she get the moon? What would happen to Kitten if she did? Where exactly is the moon, anyway? Use these questions to find out how much children understand about the moon.

After the Story

Children will be relieved when Kitten gets home and is finally able to drink a bowl of milk. Share a rewarding cup of milk with each child and congratulate children on finishing the story.

Language Arts Connections

"Poor Kitten!"

For younger children, work on fluency by pointing out the repeating phrase, "Poor Kitten!" Have children say it after you. Then, reread the story. Each time you reach this phrase, let children repeat it with you, sounding more and more sympathetic each time.

Math Connections

Calendar Math

Use the lunar calendar to inspire calendar math. Photocopy a large, blank calendar page. Fill in the dates of the current month. Then, look in your local newspaper or online to find out when the moon will be new, first quarter (half moon with the left side dark), full, and last or third quarter (half moon with the right side dark).

Copy and cut out the Moon Phase Patterns (page 53). Position the moons on the calendar to correspond with where the moon phases will fall during the month. Then, ask children questions like, "How many days are between the last quarter and the new moon?" "How many days are between the full moon and the new moon?" "If today is the 13th, in how many days will we see the first quarter moon?" If children are old enough, write out the questions and prepare an answer key to make the activity self-checking. You may want to prepare another set with different questions so that pairs of children can quiz each other.

Science Connections

Learn about the Moon

Many young children are fascinated by the moon. Talk about why on some nights the moon is round, like Kitten's full moon and, on other nights, it looks like it has been cut in half or is thin like a fingernail. Explain that the moon goes around the earth each month, which means that sometimes the moon is between the sun and the earth. When this happens, the sun cannot shine on the part of the moon that is facing the earth, so the moon looks dark to us. To demonstrate this phenomenon, have one child hold a flashlight and be the sun. Have another child stand in front of the "sun" and be the earth. Have a third child be the moon and walk slowly around the earth, always facing it.

Point out that one-half of the moon always has light on it, but the earth can only see the dark half when the moon is between the earth and the sun. Add to the experience by taking children outside when the moon is visible during the day to observe the moon's shape and where it is in the sky.

Problem-Solving and Social Skills Connections

Setting Goals

Kitten does not get the exact reward she plans on (the milk in the sky), but she is rewarded. Explain that Kitten has a goal, which means there is something she really wants and will work very hard to get. Tell children you are going to set a goal for them, and they will get a reward when they reach that goal as a class. Choose a goal that is pertinent to your classroom and that children will support, such as no grabbing away toys for one day (for young children) or learning the alphabet or numbers 1–10 (for older children). Talk about what you will do to help them. Then, set a class reward such as a special snack or a little party.

Each day, help children measure how close they are to the goal using a scale that suits the goal you have chosen. When children finally reach the goal, present the reward. Make sure children understand why they are being rewarded and how they all contributed.

Fine Motor Connections

Drinking Milk

Show children the next-to-last page of the story with Kitten drinking a bowl of milk. Ask children if they had a bowl of milk, if this is how they would drink it. Expect a resounding chorus of "Nooo!" Let children offer suggestions for how they would drink milk from a bowl if they couldn't have it in a cup; then, suggest that a bowl of milk is a lot like a bowl of soup. Let a volunteer explain how to eat soup. (Very young children often do not get to eat soup because it is messy, so you or a child who is capable may need to demonstrate.) Then, give each child a small bowl of milk, a napkin, and a spoon. Let children practice carefully spooning up the milk and eating it from the spoon. If children prove to be good at this, reward them with another treat in a bowl, such as chicken soup, applesauce, or pudding.

Gross Motor Connections

How Do Kittens Move?

Kitten is a very active animal. Over the course of the book, she climbs, jumps, tumbles, leaps, races, and more. Children will love to learn the meaning of these action words by doing them. Take children outside or into an open indoor area. Before you begin to read the book, tell them to listen carefully for the action words in the story. As you read, children should start by closing their eyes and stretching their necks and licking the air. Then, they should wiggle their bottoms, leap into the air (instead of off the stairs), and tumble to the ground. Other action scenes include chasing the moon, climbing a tree (substitute a piece of playground equipment), racing around, leaping again (this time into a pond), and walking.

Art Connections

Make Our Own Moons

Let each child make their very own moon. First, show children a variety of photographs of the moon, including pictures that reveal the craters. Next, provide a large circle for children to trace around, such as a pot lid or a plastic food storage container. Let children trace their circles on butcher paper and cut them out. Children can paint their moons with glow-in-the-dark paint (available from home improvement and craft supply stores). Then, to make the moons more realistic, provide smaller circular objects that can be used as stamps, such as bottle caps, milk jug lids, and the rims of plastic cups. Let children dip the circles in gray paint and make craters on their moons. (If you have studied moon phases, children may also want to make crescent moons or quarter moons.) Display the moons around your classroom. Occasionally dim the lights to observe the glow-in-the-dark effects.

Creative Dramatics Connections

Visit the Moon

Children already know it is impossible to walk to the moon, so ask them how else they think they might get there. After some discussion, explain that one way to get to the moon is by rocket ship! Show pictures of spaceships and talk about the fact that astronauts have visited the moon. Then, "visit" the moon yourself! Arrange chairs in two long rows and have children sit in them as you pretend to blast off into space, making sure to bump during liftoff and feel the weightlessness of space as you exit the atmosphere. Bounce around on the moon, which has one-sixth of earth's gravity; then, head back to the spaceship.

Be a Kitten

Younger children may enjoy the warmth and comfort of pretending with animals. Provide (empty) bowls of milk, soft bedding, and plenty of stuffed kittens and cats. Let children spend time pretending to be and to care for these sometimes calm, sometimes playful animals.

Moon Phase Patterns

Directions are found on page 51.

New Moon

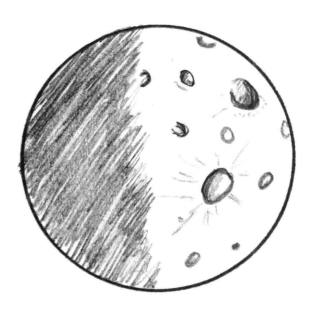

First Quarter

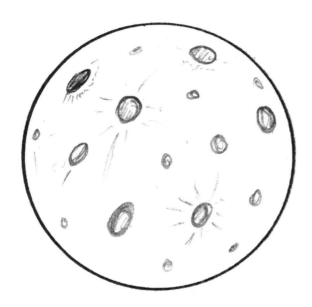

Full Moon

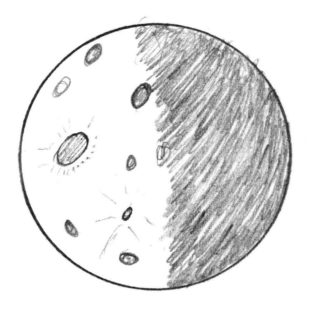

Last Quarter

Name _____

What Does Kitten Look Like?

Directions: The kitten in the story is drawn in black and white. Color the kitten below to show how you think Kitten would look in color.

MAKE WAY FOR DUCKLINGS

Written and illustrated
by Robert McCloskey
Copyright 1969, Viking Press

Story Summary

Mr. and Mrs. Mallard search for a home in Boston. They find a suitable nesting site on a small island in the Charles River, but chaos ensues when the parents decide to move their ducklings to the Public Garden because they have to cross the intersections of so many busy streets. With the help of the police department, the Mallards successfully move their ducklings and settle in to their new home.

Themes:
- safety
- community and geography
- science and nature

Skills:
- word families
- number words
- biology
- traffic safety

Vocabulary:
bank, beckoned, bursting, delighted, dither, enormous, flapped, hatched, horrid, molt, opposite, pond, pride, responsibility, satisfied, waddled

Related Books:
Blueberries for Sal
by Robert McCloskey
(Viking, 1948)

Five Little Ducks
by Raffi
(Crown, 1999)

Before the Story

Ask children if they have ever seen ducks. Discuss some facts children know about ducks, such as they fly and swim, they lay eggs, the babies are called ducklings, etc. Ask children what they think might happen when ducks live in the middle of a busy city.

During the Story

As you read, ask the children about each possible living space. What do they think would be good about living in the Public Garden? What might make the Public Garden a bad place for a family of ducks to live? What are good and bad things about living on an island in the Charles River?

After the Story

Ask children if they think Mr. and Mrs. Mallard did a good job of raising a family. What could they have done differently? Then, ask children to think of ways that Mr. and Mrs. Mallard acted like their own parents.

Language Arts Connections

Rhyming Words

Children will hear the word endings /ack/ and /uck/ often in this story. As you read the book, emphasize these two sounds in the words *ducklings, quacked, Jack, Kack, Lack, Mack, Nack, Ouack, Pack, Quack,* and *ducks*. Then, have children help you make a list of words with the ending /ack/ (*back, clack, crack, hack, rack, tack, whack*) and the ending /uck/ (*buck, cluck, luck, muck, puck, stuck, truck,* and *tuck*). Include the rhyming words from the story, as well. Then, read words from the list in random order. When children hear the /ack/ ending, they should quack like ducks. When they hear the /uck/ ending, they should say, "Lucky ducks!"

Math Connections

Lucky Ducks

Use the game Lucky Ducks as a math activity. Provide eight rubber ducks to match the number of ducklings in the story. Attach a strip of masking tape to the bottom of each duck and use a permanent marker to write a numeral from 1 to 8 on each. On a few plastic place mats, write the corresponding number words in order in a straight line.

Place the ducks in a tub of water or on a large piece of blue paper. Let children pick up the ducks, look at their numbers, and line them up in order on the plastic mats by matching the numerals to the number words. If you do not want to teach number words, simply let children line up the ducks in numerical order.

Science Connections

Webbed Feet

Talk about the period of time where both Mr. and Mrs. Mallard molt (lose their feathers) and have to rely on walking and swimming. This explains why they must be in a safe place; they and their ducklings cannot fly to safety. Then, look at the drawings of the ducks' feet; discuss how webbed feet make it easier to swim. Let children test whether webbed feet work better than feet with separate toes to move water. Explain that the more water a foot (or paddle) moves, the harder it is to move the paddle through the water and the larger the waves it makes. Fill a large tub halfway with water. Provide two rubber gloves. Leave one glove as is but use waterproof glue to attach together the fingers of the other glove. When the glue is dry, let children take turns putting their hands in the gloves and paddling. Ask which glove makes bigger waves and which glove is harder to push through the water. Let children try to explain in their own words why one would be better for swimming.

Problem-Solving and Social Skills Connections

Where Should the Ducks Live?

Combine the story of the Mallard family with an exploration of basic needs and habitat. Reread the story and help children make a list of things that are important to the Mallard family when choosing a home for their ducklings. They need shelter (a place to build a nest), a safe environment (no foxes, turtles, or wheeled vehicles until the ducklings are old enough to avoid them), adequate food (either natural sources or a good feeding ground), and a water source (because ducks swim to find food and need water to drink and to clean themselves).

Provide a map of your community. Point out places where ducks might be able to live safely, citing availability of the listed requirements. Then, if you can, take children to visit a place where you know ducks reside.

If you cannot make a field trip, then provide a large piece of butcher paper and let children plan, draw, and color a perfect duck habitat for your community.

Fine Motor Connections

Hard-Boiled Eggs

Use eggs to improve fine-motor skills and provide a nutritious snack. Before the activity, boil one egg for each child. (Eggs that are two weeks old may be easier to peel than very fresh eggs.) Place eggs in a pot, cover with water to one inch over the eggs, and turn the heat to high. When the water reaches a rolling boil, immediately turn down the heat and simmer the eggs for about 10 minutes. Begin the activity by telling children that not all eggs hatch into ducklings (or chicks, for that matter). Ask how easy or difficult children think it was for the ducklings to break out of the eggs. Give each child a cooled, boiled egg and help them carefully peel it under cold, running water. Discard the shells. Then, either slice, salt, and eat the eggs or mash them with mayonnaise, salt, pepper, and a little vinegar to make egg salad. Spread on bread and enjoy!

Caution: Before completing any food activity, ask families' permission and inquire about students' food allergies and religious or other food preferences.

Gross Motor Connections

Walking in a Line

When you read the sections of the book where the ducklings are walking in a line through traffic, ask if anyone can explain why it is safer to walk in a line. Tell children that the policemen can easily see where the line of ducklings begins and ends, so he knows when it is safe to let the traffic resume. Have children practice walking in a straight, orderly line. Line up children alphabetically by their first names (like the ducklings in the story) and go on a long walk through the school and on the grounds. Practice stopping and waiting, even if there is no traffic. Periodically remind children to be quiet in line, to pay attention, and to keep their hands to themselves. When you return to the classroom, reward children with duck-shaped candy or marshmallows, if they are available, or with chocolate "eggs."

Art Connections

Hatching Ducklings

Let children "hatch" their own ducklings. First, make a nest using strips of paper or cloth in a basket. Provide a plastic egg for each child. Then, let each child draw and color a picture of the contents of a raw egg. (Crack a raw chicken egg into a bowl and let children observe it as they draw.) Have each child place their drawing inside their plastic egg, write their name on the egg, and place it in the basket. After children leave for the day, copy the Duckling Patterns (page 58) on yellow card stock and cut them out. Make one duckling for each child. Open each child's plastic egg and replace the egg drawing with a duckling. The next day, let children open their eggs to find their ducklings. Children may decorate the ducklings by gluing on tiny yellow feathers and wiggly eyes.

Creative Dramatics Connections

Obey the Rules

The ducks stay safe even on a busy street because they obey Michael the policeman and wait for him to tell them when it is safe to cross. Children must also obey traffic and pedestrian laws. Make a stop sign on red card stock and cut it out. Use strips of masking tape on the floor to create an intersection.

Assign some children to be ducks, some to be motorists, and one to be the police officer. (You may want to be the police officer yourself until children get the hang of this activity.) Use a whistle, the stop sign, and hand gestures to indicate which group gets to cross and which group must wait their turn.

Duckling Patterns

Directions are found on page 57.

Eggs in the Nest

Directions: Not all duck families are the same size. Draw a line to match each pair of nests with the same number of eggs and ducklings.

Miss Bindergarten Gets Ready for Kindergarten

Written by Joseph Slate
Illustrated by Ashley Wolff
Copyright 2001, Puffin Books

Story Summary

As each of the children in her class get ready for the first day of kindergarten, Miss Bindergarten rushes to make her classroom perfect. The children meet with various mishaps and do the typical "getting ready" things while Miss Bindergarten transforms her drab, empty classroom into an inviting arena for learning.

Themes:
- school
- routine
- being prepared

Skills:
- alphabet
- rhyming
- measurement
- biology
- preparedness

Vocabulary:
cocoa, fights, kindergarten, puddle, sneaker, sneaks

Related Books:
First Day Jitters
by Julie Danneberg
(Charlesbridge, 2000)

The Night Before Kindergarten
by Natasha Wing
(Grosset & Dunlap, 2001)

Before the Story

Ask children what they do to get ready for school each day. Then, ask, "What did you do to get ready for the *first* day of school? How is the first day of school different?" Finish by telling children about your setup time and explain that the book is about the things a teacher and her students do to get ready for the first day of school.

During the Story

As you read about each child in Miss Bindergarten's class getting ready, invite children to raise their hands each time they hear you read about something that they, too, do to get ready for school.

After the Story

Take children on a little tour of your classroom as you look at the pictures of Miss Bindergarten's classroom. Help them point out things that are found in both rooms. Talk about whether the things are exactly the same.

Language Arts Connections

Alphabetical Order

Miss Bindergarten's classroom is filled with animal students—each one beginning with a different letter of the alphabet. Turn to the last page of the book and share the class picture with children. Assign each child a character from the book and have them line up in alphabetical order as you call their characters' names. Do this two or three times if needed to cover all of the letters in the alphabet.

Finish the Sentence

Work on rhyming and word recognition. After you have read the book a few times, read all of the words in each phrase except for the last word, allowing children to finish the sentence. For example, read,

"Patricia Packer sneaks a ——."

and let children fill in the missing word.

Math Connections

How Tall Are You?

Before beginning this activity, put a measurement chart up in the classroom. On one of the pages depicting Miss Bindergarten's preparations, point out to children that she is measuring the height of her cockatoo. Measure children and record their heights in inches on the chart. Then, choose two children and compare both the numerals of their heights in inches and where the students' heights are recorded on the chart. Help students understand the correlation between the greater numeral also being the taller height. Let children practice measuring other things in the classroom using rulers or tape measures. Help them measure and compare their feet, tables, books, and so on, discovering that longer objects also have larger numerals that represent the greater number of inches.

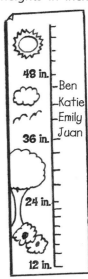

Science Connections

Learn about Animals

Children will be very interested in the parade of animals that prepares to enter Miss Bindergarten's classroom. Play an animal matching game using the Animal Match cards (pages 63–65). Make two copies of each page. Color, cut out, and laminate for durability. Let the children play memory match with the cards or simply enjoy laying them all out on the floor and finding the pairs of matching cards.

For a challenge, hand each child an animal card and help them line up alphabetically.

Problem-Solving and Social Skills Connections

Be Prepared

Miss Bindergarten's classroom looks wonderful and organized. The students seem excited and happy to be there—even sad little Ian has found a book he likes. Read children the self-stick notes on the title page that Miss Bindergarten uses to make sure she gets everything done. Talk about how differently the first day of school would have turned out if she had not gotten up on time or had forgotten things she was supposed to bring to the classroom. Then, ask children how they can be prepared like Miss Bindergarten. If you have a class project, program, or field trip coming up, let children help you brainstorm a list of things that must be done beforehand, like sending home permission slips, getting them signed and returned, collecting money, packing lunches, and more. Post the list. As each task is accomplished, let a child check it off. Hopefully, your event will be organized and trouble free!

Fine Motor Connections

Tie Your Shoes

Show the page with Ursula Crewe, who is tying her shoe. Do all of the children in your classroom know how to tie their shoes? If not, have a shoe-tying lesson. Bring in as many kid-sized sneakers as you can find, since many children wear shoes with buckles or hook-and-loop tape. Put the shoes on dolls and children. Demonstrate for small groups how to tie a shoe using these steps:

1. Start by crossing the laces.
2. Wrap one lace around the other.
3. Pull the laces tight and make a loop in one lace.
4. Wrap the other lace around the loop.
5. Pull that lace through the wrapped overlap to make another loop.
6. Pull on both of the loops to tighten the bow.

It may also be helpful to have a "how to put on your shoes" session since some children may have a difficult time getting their feet into their shoes.

What Would You Bring to School?

Copy page 66 for each child. Explain to children that they can decide what they will put in their backpacks by coloring and cutting out the school tools at the bottom of the page and then pasting them on the backpacks.

Gross Motor Connections

Rainy Day Fun

This is a great rainy-day gross motor activity. Point out pages where Miss Bindergarten puts books on the shelf and sorts blocks into bins and where she has gathered children into a circle. Before school the next day, remove blocks and books from bins and shelves. (Leave one block in each bin so that children know where to sort them.) Make sure the items are either on the floor or a high shelf so that children must bend or stretch to reach them. Then, have a sort-and-stack relay. Line up children in two teams. Play some upbeat music. When you say, "Go," the first child in each line should race to the books and place three neatly on the shelf, then go to the blocks and sort five blocks into the correct bins, and then run to sit in the circle in front of you like Miss Bindergarten's students at the end of the book. When all children have finished the race, reward them by reading a favorite book. If you want to have a winner, let the last runner on the winning team choose the book.

Art Connections

Mobiles

Show children the page where Miss Bindergarten is hanging the whale mobile and also look at the picture of the finished classroom which shows two additional mobiles in it. If possible, display a few examples of mobiles in your own classroom. Then, provide yarn, craft sticks, paper clips, and art supplies. Let each child create small pieces of artwork for their own mobiles. You can assign a theme from the ones shown in the book (shapes, ocean mammals, and space) or let children choose their own themes. If possible, laminate each piece of art before punching a hole in it.

Then, help children pull a length of yarn through each hole and tie or attach it with a paper clip. Tie the other ends of the yarn around the craft sticks and attach the sticks together to make a mobile. If possible, hang the mobiles around the classroom or string a clothesline and hang the mobiles from it.

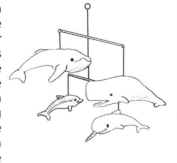

Creative Dramatics Connections

School Bus

Many young children have never ridden a school bus. Make a school bus in your classroom. Ask for a donation of a cardboard refrigerator box. Cut the side off of the box and decorate it to look like the side of a school bus. Cut out windows and a door opening; then, paint the box yellow and decorate it with black paper letters and white and red circles (lights). Place chairs inside the bus, including a larger chair next to the door for the driver. If possible, make a steering wheel for the bus by attaching a plastic foam block to a table and placing it in front of the driver's chair. Then, use a real steering wheel or make one from heavy cardboard. (Punch a hole in the center of the cardboard wheel.) Push a long bolt through the hole in the wheel into the plastic foam, deep enough to hold the steering wheel in place but leaving enough space for the wheel to turn freely. When the bus is complete, let children take turns playing on it. Occasionally, take a turn playing the part of the bus driver.

Animal Match

Directions:

Make two copies of pages 63–65, color, cut out, and laminate for durability.

Let the children play memory match with the cards or simply enjoy laying them all out on the floor and finding the pairs of matching cards.

alligator

beaver

cat

dog

elephant

frog

gorilla

hippopotamus

Animal Match

iguana

jaguar

kangaroo

lion

moose

newt

otter

pig

quokka

Animal Match

rhinoceros	squirrel	tiger
vakari monkey	vole	wolf
xenosaurus	yak	zebra

What Would You Bring to School?

Directions: Color the school tools at the bottom of page. Cut them out and glue them on the backpack.

GLUE

CRAYONS

The Mitten

Adapted and illustrated
by Jan Brett
Copyright 1989
G. P. Putnam's Sons

Story Summary

Little Nicki asks his grandmother to knit him a pair of snow-white mittens. She warns him that he will lose them in the snow, but he insists, and she finally obliges. Sure enough, Nicki drops a mitten, which then becomes a shelter for animals who crawl inside to make themselves warm. When Nicki finds the mitten again and takes it home, his grandmother discovers that the mitten has mysteriously stretched to several times its original size.

Themes:
- responsibility
- compromise
- winter
- wild animals

Skills:
- vocabulary
- /ed/ word endings
- number sentences
- biology

Vocabulary:
attracted, bulged, burrowed, commotion, diggers, glinty, investigate, jostled, kickers, prickles, snowshoe, swooped, talons, tunneling

Related Books:
The Hat
by Jan Brett
(Putnam, 1997)

The Umbrella
by Jan Brett
(Putnam, 2004)

Before the Story

Ask children how many of them have played in the snow. (Depending on where you live, the answers should be obvious, unless children in a warm climate have traveled in winter.) Talk about what a mitten is and bring in a pair to show children. Pass them around for children to try on.

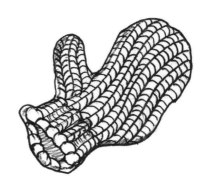

During the Story

Draw special attention to the side panel illustrations. Each one shows what is happening with characters that are not in the main illustration. Some of these characters have not yet been introduced in the story at the time they are shown in the side panels. Ask children what they think will happen next as they look at each side panel to see the actions of characters that are not in the main picture.

After the Story

Ask children what they think would have happened if the bear had not sneezed and the animals had not been blown out of the mitten. Do they think Nicki would have found his mitten anyway? Why or why not?

Language Arts Connections

Animal Words

New animal vocabulary is an important part of understanding this book. It is helpful that the author explains a little about each animal and why the others decide to let that animal crowd into the mitten. Enlarge and display the Animal Patterns (page 71) on a chalkboard. Have children study the animal pictures to answer the question, "Why should I let you in?" Record children's answers next to each animal's picture.

Wanted

Many verbs in this book have an /ed/ ending. Write these story verbs on the board: *want, warn, finish, drop, burrow, stop, disappear, swoop, appear, start, swell, stretch, scatter,* and *look.* For the first verb, say, "Today, I want. Yesterday, I _____." Children should respond, "Wanted!" Repeat for all of the story's verbs. Then, write each present tense verb on an index card and *ed* on another card. Let children practice putting the /ed/ ending index card next to the present tense verbs and saying the new past tense verbs.

Math Connections

Counting Animals

Use the Animal Patterns (page 71) for a counting activity. Enlarge, cut out, and laminate one set of animal patterns. On a sheet of poster board, enlarge and trace the Mitten Pattern (page 70). The mitten should be larger than the largest animal. Cut it out and then use it as a template to trace a back for the mitten. Laminate both mittens and staple the edges of the patterns together, leaving the wrist open to form a pocket. Sit with a pair of children at a table. Ask a child to place two animals into the mitten. Write the numeral 2 on a sheet of paper. Then, ask him to put three more animals into the mitten. Write + 3 next to the 2. Have the other child remove and count the animals. Write = 5 on the paper to complete the number sentence. Repeat to create several other number sentences. As children master the counting and addition skills, change the activity to make subtraction sentences by having children remove animals from the mitten.

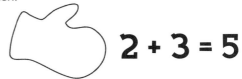

$$2 + 3 = 5$$

Science Connections

Real Animals

Did you know that hedgehogs purr when they are happy? Or that owls eat their prey whole and spit out the fur and bones in balls called *pellets*? Help children learn about each of the animals in the story. Provide books about the animals listed or help children research them on the Internet. What do the animals eat in the winter? Do some of these animals hibernate? Enlarge, cut out, and post the drawings of the animals from the Animal Patterns (page 71). Let each child choose one animal to study. (Make several sets of copies if there are more children in the class than animals.) Help children research interesting facts about the animals they chose. Each day for eight days, set aside a few minutes to talk about one of the animals. Enlarge, copy, and hand out to each child the pattern for the animal you are talking about that day. Have children color the animals and help them write some facts about that animal on the back of the pattern.

Problem-Solving and Social Skills Connections

Be Responsible

Before beginning this activity, purchase mittens from a thrift store or ask parents for donations. Remind children that Baba warns Nicki about losing his mittens because they are white like the snow, and sure enough, he loses one.

Ask whether Baba should have made the white mittens Nicki wanted. What could Nicki have done to keep from losing his mitten? Let children make suggestions for how Nicki could have been more responsible and discuss why it is important not to lose things. Then, on a Friday, give each child a mitten (or a pair if you have enough). Explain that each child will be responsible, like Nicki, for keeping up with their mitten, and each child must bring their mitten back to school on Monday. Send home the Mitten Note (page 71) so that parents know about and can help with the assignment. On Monday, see which children were able to keep up with their mittens and ask how they did it.

Fine Motor Connections

Lacing Cards

Work with mitten-shaped lacing cards. Copy the Mitten Pattern (page 70) onto colorful card stock and laminate it. Punch holes about half an inch from the edge around the perimeter of the mitten. Provide lengths of yarn for children to lace in and out of the holes. For a more challenging activity, punch more holes in the center of the mitten as well as around the outside edge. Provide variegated yarn and let children "knit" their own mittens.

Stuffed Mittens

To give children fine-motor practice as well as something to take home, give each child two copies of the Mitten Pattern (page 70) to color. Laminate the patterns, place them one on top of the other, and punch holes in them. Let children lace the two patterns together with yarn, leaving them open at the wrist. Let children stuff their mittens with cotton balls or shredded newspaper and then lace the mittens closed.

Gross Motor Connections

Mitten Race

Oh no! Nicki has lost his mitten! Have a race to help him find it. Before class, reserve the playground and hide donated mittens or copies of the Mitten Pattern (page 70) around the area. Make sure you hide enough for each child to have a chance to find at least one. Place a basket in the center of the playground and challenge children to find all of the mittens as quickly as possible. When you say, "Go!" children must race to find the mittens as fast as they can. Each time a mitten is found, the child must return to the basket and drop it in before running off to look for another one. When all of the mittens have been found, reward children with something else to warm their hands—cups of hot chocolate.

Art Connections

Decorate Mittens

Give children a chance to work with fabrics and trims and express themselves with different media. Enlarge a copy of the Mitten Pattern (page 70) on card stock for each child. Also, provide scraps of fabric, sequins, pom-poms, lace, ribbons, buttons, and glue. Let children use all of the materials to decorate their mittens as elaborately as they wish. Write their names on the backs of the mittens and display them on a bulletin board titled, "We won't lose our mittens in the snow!"

To "test" which mittens are most easily found, remove them from the bulletin board after class at the end of the day and hide them around the classroom. Then, invite children to go on a "mitten hunt" the next morning.

Creative Dramatics Connections

Experience "The Mitten"

Children will be fascinated by the aspect of animals crowding into a small mitten and will be eager to do it themselves. Let children try this experiment to see if they can accomplish the same thing. Provide a large appliance box and decorate it to look like a mitten. (Using a box is safer than using anything made of fabric.) Have children remove shoes and bulky clothing. Place the box on its side on a mat. Line children up and assign each of them an animal from the story. The first child should be a mole, the second should be a hare, and so on.

Let children take turns trying to squeeze into the box like the animals, until eight children (or as many as possible) are in the box. Monitor the activity so that all children are safe and enjoying the experiment and everyone has a chance to try to fit into the box.

Mitten Pattern
Directions are found on pages 68 and 69.

Mitten Note

Dear Parents,

   We have been reading the story *The Mitten* by Jan Brett. In this story, Nicki loses a mitten that his grandmother knit for him. Our class has talked about how important it is to take care of our belongings. Starting this Friday, I have asked all of the children in the class to "babysit" a mitten for the weekend. The mitten needs to go everywhere your child goes, and your child needs to be as responsible as possible for keeping up with it. You may help your child by brainstorming ideas for how to keep the mitten safe. On Monday, please send the mitten back to school with your child, and we will talk about how the class kept track of their mittens. There are no consequences for losing a mitten; it is just a learning exercise. Good luck!

Sincerely,

_____

Animal Patterns Directions are found on page 68.

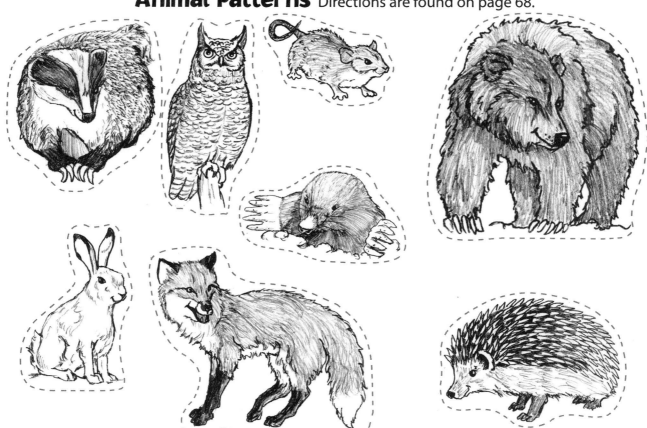

THE NAPPING HOUSE

Written by Audrey Wood
Illustrated by Don Wood
Copyright 1984
Harcourt, Inc.

Story Summary

In this cumulative story, a granny, a child, a dog, a cat, and a mouse are all rudely awakened in a chain reaction caused by the bite of a tiny flea. Fortunately, the heavy rain chooses this time to stop, and all members of the household seem perfectly happy to be awake and outside.

Themes:
- naps
- chain reaction
- home and family

Skills:
- /ing/ word endings (gerunds)
- vocabulary
- ordinal numbers
- biology

Vocabulary:
claws, cozy, dozing, granny, slumbering, snoozing, thumps, wakeful

Related Books:
Silly Sally
by Audrey Wood
(Red Wagon Books, 1999)

Just a Nap
by Mercer Mayer
(Golden Books, 1989)

Before the Story

Talk about taking naps. Ask for a show of hands of children that still take naps. Ask them if they like to take naps in a bed or somewhere else and if they have any pets that sleep with them.

During the Story

On each page, the animals are less and less hidden as it nears each animal's turn to join the pile on the bed. The positions of the mouse and the flea are especially interesting because they are small and often hard to see. Challenge children to find the mouse and the flea on each page. Also, point out what is happening outside of the window on each page.

After the Story

Ask children if they know what a flea looks like and if any of their pets have ever had fleas. Have they ever been bitten by a flea or any other bug? Did it hurt? Do they think a bite from a bug would wake them up? What can they do to avoid being bitten by bugs?

Language Arts Connections

Bells and Phonemic Awareness

Ask children what sound a bell makes. Chances are someone will say, "Ring ring!" Write the word *ring* on the board. Ask children what sound they hear at the end of the word. Explain that many words in this book end with /ing/ and that /ing/ at the end of a word often means an action is happening. Point out the many examples of /ing/ words in the story. Then, give each child a bell. (Sets of bells are available at discount stores and craft supply stores.) Tell children that each time they hear a word that has an /ing/ ending, they should ring their bells.

Pantomime Sleeping Words

There are many words for sleeping in this story. On the board, write the words *sleeping*, *napping*, *snoring*, *dreaming*, *dozing*, *snoozing*, and *slumbering*. Help children learn and understand these words. Comment on subtle differences between the meanings of the words. Then, read each word aloud one at a time. Let children act out each word as you read it.

Math Connections

Ordinal Numbers

Use the Napping House Patterns (page 75) to teach ordinal numbers in a fun way. Cut out each figure and glue it to the lid of a different-sized box. For example, glue the flea to a ring box, the mouse to an individual serving size cereal box, the cat to a child's shoe box, the dog to a large cereal box, the child to a small shirt box, and the granny to a large shirt box or a boot box. (You can enlarge the patterns proportionally to different sizes, if desired.) Tape the lids on the boxes and place the boxes next to a table. Reread the book to a small group and tell children to stack the boxes in the same order as the sleeping characters. Ask, "Who is sleeping in the bed first?" One child should select the box with the granny and place it on the table. Repeat, using ordinal numbers, until the first five characters are stacked on the table. When you add the flea, shout, "Wakeful flea!" and let children demolish the pile of boxes. Repeat the activity and let children prompt each other with the ordinal numbers.

Science Connections

Real Fleas

Read the children factual information about "real" fleas. After the children have listened to the information ask them to draw a picture of what they think a real flea would look like. When the children have finished drawing their pictures, compare them to real photographs of fleas. How are their pictures similar to the photographs? How are they different?

For teacher reference: Fleas are small [1/16 to 1/8-inch (1.5 to 3.3 mm) long]. They are dark colored, wingless insects with drinking straw-like mouthparts. Their bodies are flattened side to side which permits easy movement through hairs or feathers. Their legs are long, the hind pair well adapted for jumping. Some fleas can jump up to seven inches vertically (18 cm) and thirteen inches horizontally (33 cm).

The flea body is hard, polished, and covered with many hairs. Its tough body is able to withstand great pressure, likely an adaptation to be able to survive scratching. Even hard squeezing between the fingers is often not enough to kill a flea. It may be necessary to crush them between the fingernails.

Problem-Solving and Social Skills Connections

Special Grandparents

Let children talk about their special relationships with their grandparents. Tell children to look at the pictures of the granny. Ask children what a granny is and if anyone calls a family member by that name. Then, let children share all of the names they call their grandparents. List the names on the board. After you have made the list, write each name in a sentence at the top of a sheet of drawing paper and give the papers to the appropriate children. For example, write "This is Cody's grandpa." Let each child draw a picture of his Nana, Grandma, Graddy, and/or Pops.

Tell children that their pictures should show them doing something fun with their grandparents. Bind the pages into a book. Read the book to the class taking time to let each of the children help you read their page and tell about their picture. If a child does not have grandparents, encourage her to substitute other family members.

Fine Motor Connections

Sequencing

To make this an activity children can do themselves, record yourself reading *The Napping House*. During the recording, pause for a few seconds as each character climbs into or jumps out of bed. Copy and color a set of the Napping House Patterns (page 75). Cut out the patterns and then laminate them. Hang a clothesline in the classroom about 2' (0.6 m) off the ground and 4' (1.2 m) long. (You can do this by tying each end of the line to opposite sides of a wooden crate.) Provide a set of the patterns along with paper clips, binder clips, or clothespins.

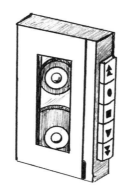

As children listen to the recording of the story, they should use the clips or clothespins to attach the patterns to the line in the order the characters are mentioned. After the flea makes its appearance, children will have to work quickly to unclip the patterns.

Gross Motor Connections

"Wakeful Flea"

One reason that this story is so appealing to children is because of the wild ruckus at the end. Play a game called "Wakeful Flea" to celebrate the ruckus. Take children outside and let them move around until you say, "Napping house!" Children should then freeze where they are, shut their eyes, and pretend to sleep until you call out, "Wakeful flea!" At this point, children should jump around wildly like the characters in the story. (You may want to revisit the book for inspiration.) Let a child who is very demonstrative be the next person to call out, "Napping house!" and "Wakeful flea!" Repeat until each child has had a turn to cue the action.

Art Connections

Rain-and-Shine House Portraits

Point out that on the first page, heavy rain is falling on the napping house, and there are few colors in the picture. On the last page, the sun is shining, and there are many brighter colors. Have children make rain-and-shine house portraits. Give each child two copies of the House Pattern (page 76). Before they begin, explain that the house itself must remain basically the same colors in both of their pictures. First, provide blue, gray, black, and dark green crayons. Play a recording of rain sound effects as each child colors one picture with the darker colors.

Then, change to a recording of birds singing and let children color their second pictures with brighter colors, including yellows, reds, and oranges. Next, have children use diluted gray watercolor paint to cover the rainy paintings and very pale, blue paint to cover the sunny ones. The paint will not affect the crayon but the white areas will be tinted.

Creative Dramatics Connections

Role Playing

This story is irresistible for role-playing. Assign children to act out each character in the story. In place of a bed, provide an open sleeping bag on the floor. (Leaving the sleeping bag open will ensure that children can remain in close quarters without having to climb on top of each other.) Let each character gather around the sleeping bag. The child who is the granny should curl up on the sleeping bag before play begins; then, other characters should follow one by one as you read the story. Instead of having a child actually play the flea, tie a small, paper flea to the end of a piece of string. When it is time for the wakeful flea to appear, have a child dangle the flea over the child who is pretending to be the mouse. At this point, all of the children should jump up in reverse order. Children will enjoy making the sleeping sounds of the characters, and they are sure to increase the drama of the awakening as much as possible.

Napping House Patterns

Directions are found on pages 73 and 74.

House Pattern

Directions: Follow your teacher's directions to make a napping house and a wakeful house.

OLIVIA

Written and illustrated
by Ian Falconer
Copyright 2000
Atheneum Books for Young Readers

Story Summary

Olivia is the introductory book in a series about a pig who enjoys life. She dresses up, makes sand castles, tries on all of the clothes in her closet, and deals with her mother, the cat, and her little brother Ian. She also appreciates the fine arts, which makes this a terrific book to use in school.

Themes:
• independence
• fine arts
• home and family

Skills:
• fluency
• counting
• scientific method
• chemistry
• self-help skills

Vocabulary:
copying, museum, prepared, wear out

Related Books:
Olivia Forms a Band
by Ian Falconer
(Atheneum, 2006)

Olivia Counts
by Ian Falconer
(Atheneum, 2002)

Before the Story

Introduce the book by telling children that Olivia is a pig who does many of the same things they do. Ask for a show of hands from children who have a little brother, have looked at paintings, have been to the beach and built a sand castle, and have dreamed of being a professional dancer or singer.

During the Story

In *Olivia*, the text is understated and pictures tell a lot of the story. Pause at some of the pages and ask children to describe what is happening. For example, when the story says Olivia has gotten pretty good at sand castles, ask children why the text says that and if they agree. On the page that says Olivia is not at all sleepy at nap time, ask what the picture shows her doing.

For young children, draw attention to the fact that the only color, besides black and white, is red. On each page, ask children what is red.

After the Story

Quiz children about different details of the book. Ask, "What were the two pictures Olivia painted?" (She painted an abstract painting and a picture of herself and Ian.) "What is the only pink thing in the book?" (Olivia is pink when she gets sunburned.) "What does Olivia move every morning after she gets up?" (She moves the cat.)

Language Arts Connections

Singing and Fluency

Singing is great fluency practice. It is natural for children to be able to sing words fluently since the rhythm and melody help children communicate more smoothly. Turn to the page where Olivia is singing from a songbook titled *40 Very Loud Songs*. Ask children what songs they think might be in that book. Start them out with names of familiar songs like "Bingo" and "Take Me Out to the Ball Game" by Jack Norworth and Albert Von Tilzer. Each day, choose a song from the list and write its lyrics on the board before children arrive for the day. Begin the day with a rousing version of the day's loud song, making sure children are gathered around the lyrics. For further fluency practice, copy the lyrics on paper for each child and let him record himself singing and then reading the lyrics.

Math Connections

Counting Practice

Do a math activity using the page on which Olivia sings from the book of *40 Very Loud Songs*. After making the song list in the Language Arts Connections activity (left), shift the focus of the activity to counting to 40. On chart paper, make lists of other things that are relevant to Olivia. For example, have children list 40 things she could do to wear herself out, 40 places she could move the cat, and 40 books she might like to read at bedtime. Reinforce the counting by letting children volunteer to fill in the numbers as you make the list.

After you have made a few lists of 40, let children choose some things they could make lists of 40 about, such as people they know, kinds of food, toys they likes, and so on. Let each child number their own list.

1 2 3 4 5 6 7 8 9 10
11 12 13 14 15 16 17 18 19 20
21 22 23 24 25 26 27 28 29 30
31 32 33 34 35 36 37 38 39 40

Science Connections

Building with Sand

Look at the page where Olivia has built a skyscraper out of sand. Provide two large piles of sand in a sensory table or outside in the sandbox. Both of the piles of sand should be very dry and impossible to build with. Also, provide molds that can be used for building sand castles. Then, take children to the sand and ask them to build a sand castle with the molds. When children tell you they cannot make the sand stick together, ask them what they could use to help the sand stick together. If you have enough sand, give each child a small amount to experiment with. Children may try to add glue, paint, or even sticky syrup if they have access to it. Finally, add water to the two larger piles of sand and let children build with it. Simplify the chemistry by explaining that water likes to stick together, and so water helps the grains of sand to stick together, too.

Problem-Solving and Social Skills Connections

Bedtime Routines

Olivia has her own ideas about sleeping. She twirls through her nap time and argues with her mother about how many bedtime books she gets to read. Ask children how they feel about bedtime. Do they complain about it? What are their routines? Let children write or dictate sentences about bedtime, naming one good thing and one thing that they would like to change. Then, have them draw pictures of themselves going to bed. Send children's artwork and writing home with them to spark family discussions about the rituals of bedtime.

What Are You Good At?

Spread Olivia's self-confidence among children. Reread the page that says Olivia is good at lots of things. Give each child a copy of the What Are You Good At? reproducible (page 80) and have them draw something they are good at. Post the artwork and let children describe their skills and then demonstrate the skills for each other.

Fine Motor Connections

Brushing Teeth

Olivia seems to be very independent. She is able to dress herself, brush her own teeth, and comb her own ears. Gather items to represent some of the things Olivia is able to do on her own: shoes with laces, combs, a small backpack, ear muffs, and a pair of mittens. Ask parents to send a new toothbrush to school with their child if possible.

Spend some time in the classroom helping children to practice tying shoes, putting on backpacks, putting on earmuffs and mittens, combing hair, and brushing teeth. If you have access to the supplies, let children practice putting on some of the other items of clothing, as well.

Gross Motor Connections

Olivia Will Wear You Out!

Prepare for this activity by gathering some yo-yos, jump ropes, toy hammers, a ball, and spoons and bowls. Show children the pictures on the page that says, "She is very good at wearing people out." Ask a few volunteers to stand at different stations throughout the room or outside on the playground and assign a volunteer to lead children through each one of the tasks.

Play some lively music as children take turns performing all of the things Olivia does to wear herself out: hammering pretend nails, jumping and dancing, trying to do headstands, kicking a ball, stirring with a spoon, jumping rope, and running. When children have completed all of the tasks, tell them to collapse on the floor for a little rest just like Olivia.

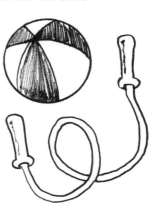

Art Connections

Paint Like the Masters

Discuss Olivia's trip to the museum. Explain the pictures she saw; one is modeled after Edgar Degas and the other after Jackson Pollock. If possible, show children examples of art by both of these artists on the Internet or in art books. Set up a Degas art station in the classroom with paper, acrylic paint, brushes, and pictures of ballet dancers. Outside, set up a Jackson Pollock area by anchoring strips of butcher paper on the ground with rocks. Provide squeeze bottles of washable paint and paintbrushes. Provide smocks or old T-shirts in both areas. As each child finishes a painting in one area, let them move to the other station. After the artwork is complete, allow it to dry. Send home the Welcome to the Gallery! invitation (page 81). To prepare for the gallery "opening," display the paintings by placing Degas-style paintings in one area and Pollock-style paintings in another and label the two areas. To create a gallery atmosphere, consider serving refreshments to families when they arrive.

Creative Dramatics Connections

Face Painting

Olivia is nothing if not dramatic. Show the picture of Olivia applying makeup. Ask if children have ever seen anyone use makeup or face paint. Their answers may include people such as women, clowns, or actors in a play. After discussion, open a face painting station. Let children choose how they would like their faces painted. (If possible, enlist help from an adult volunteer with artistic ability.) Let children spend the day with their faces painted and provide hand and wall mirrors for children to admire themselves.

My Own Mask

Show the picture of Olivia with the paper bag over her head. Ask children to describe the mask she is wearing. Give each child a paper grocery bag and art supplies to make their own mask. Tell children they can make scary masks like Olivia's in the picture, but they can also make any other kind. Over the next several days, let children wear their masks in the creative dramatics center or during free time.

What Are You Good At?

Directions: The story says Olivia is good at lots of things. So are you! List five things you are good at. Then, draw yourself below doing one of these things.

1. I am good at _____.

2. I am good at _____.

3. I am good at _____.

4. I am good at _____.

5. I am good at _____.

(Olivia)

Welcome to the Gallery!

Please join our class
and view their creative artwork.

Place: _____

Date: _____

Time: _____

Exhibition: _____

- -

(Olivia)

Welcome to the Gallery!

Please join our class
and view their creative artwork.

Place: _____

Date: _____

Time: _____

Exhibition: _____

One fish two fish
red fish blue fish

Written and illustrated
by Dr. Seuss
Copyright 1960
Beginner Books, A division of Random House

Story Summary

Although this book starts out as a description of some fish characters, it quickly changes into a series of scenarios describing many different characters, some of which are pets. All of the characters have silly names that rhyme with their descriptions. Children will be delighted with the different personalities of all the strange and wonderful Dr. Seuss creatures.

Themes:

- rhymes and word families
- personality traits
- home and family

Skills:

- word family recognition
- counting
- skip counting
- bully awareness

Vocabulary:

number words from one to eleven, box, ink, swish

Related Books:

Hop on Pop
by Dr. Seuss
(Random House, 1963)

Fox in Socks
by Dr. Seuss
(Random House, 1965)

Before the Story

Ask children to name some rhyming words. If possible, help them think of some words that rhyme with their names. Then, make up some nonsense words that rhyme, as well. See who can tell the difference between real words and nonsense words.

RHYMING NAMES & NONSENSE NAMES

Jenny - Penny - Benny - Denny - zenny

Tim - him - Jim - whim - dim - yim

Kate - gate - late - mate - plate - zrate

Mike - bike - trike - like - hike - drike

During the Story

After each small section, stop and repeat all of the rhyming words on the page. Have children repeat them after you.

After the Story

You may want to create a word wall with all of the sets of rhyming words from this book. Instead of using letters as headers, write each word-family word-ending you want to teach on an index card and use the cards as headers. Under the cards, write the appropriate word family words. Invite children to suggest other word family words for each list. You may also want to record the words Seuss invented. If so, record the regular words in black ink and then write Seuss's invented words in blue or red ink.

DR. SEUSS WORD FAMILIES

- ish	- ar	- ed	- ark
fish	car	bed	dark
dish	bar	Ned	park
wish	far	red	lark
swish	star	sled	Clark

- ad	- at	- un	- y
bad	bat	bun	by
dad	hat	sun	my
sad	fat	run	fly
had	mat	fun	try
mad	slat	gun	why

Language Arts Connections

Rhyming Antler Toss

There are many rhyming words in this book. Make learning rhyming words fun, interactive, and kinesthetic by playing a real round of Ring the Gack. On cardboard, draw the head and antlers of a Gack and cut it out. On each antler branch, draw a picture that appears in the book and that has many rhyming possibilities. Tape the Gack to the back of a chair and reinforce the antlers with craft sticks. Locate a set of plastic ringtoss hoops. You might also use plastic embroidery hoops or make hoops out of rope secured with duct tape. Let children toss the hoops at the antlers. If a child "rings" an antler, have the child say the name of the picture on that antler and then think of a word that rhymes with the picture. For example, if the hoop landed on an antler with a picture of a fish, the child might then say the rhyming word *dish* or *wish*.

It is also fun to play this game in teams. Teammates take turns tossing the hoop, but all of the team members work together to think up rhyming words.

Math Connections

Count All of the Fish

Children can do a simple counting exercise with this book. Let each child spend time with the book counting all of the fish. Explain that children should start with the fish on the first page of the story and continue until the characters change from fish to something else. (There are 19 fish in the first part of the book and 3 more fish appear much later.)

Skip Counting by Twos

For a more complex challenge, read page 12 that says, "Some have two feet, some have four." Since the feet are counted two, four, and six, teach children to count by twos. Copy and cut out the Caterpillars and Feet Patterns (page 85). You will need to make multiple copies of the feet. Line up the caterpillars on the board and add feet to each caterpillar. Start with just two feet, then four, then six, then eight, and so on. Just by looking at the number of feet on each caterpillar and saying the numbers in order, children will count by twos.

Science Connections

Describe a Suess Creature

There are many new creatures in this book that children will want to know more about. Since that information was known only to Dr. Seuss, help children make up their own facts and information about the creatures. Let each child choose a creature in the book and write or dictate answers to the following questions. Adjust the questions' content or the wording according to the ages of the children in your classroom.

1. Is the creature a mammal, reptile, fish, insect, or bird? How do you know?
2. What does this creature eat?
3. In what part of the world does this creature live?
4. Does this creature live in trees? Underground? On land? In the water?
5. Is this creature common or endangered?

After each child answers these questions, let them draw a picture of a family of the creature. Post the pictures of the creatures with their corresponding facts.

Problem-Solving and Social Skills Connections

Don't Be a Bully!

Use this book as a springboard to discuss bullying. Show the page where the very, very bad fish is pushing the other fish. Ask children if they would like to be friends with the fish who is doing the pushing. Why or why not? Explain that the red fish is a bully, which is someone who enjoys teasing or hurting other people. Discuss some outcomes that would improve the situation. Then, have children draw pictures of the scenarios they would like to see.

Suggest that they might draw the red fish getting into trouble for pushing the other fish, or that maybe the red fish will begin to feel bad and apologize. After the drawings are complete, choose some depictions for children to act out.

Fine Motor Connections

Finger Counting

Show children the character on page 16 of the book counting his fingers. Note that he has eleven fingers: seven on one hand and four on the other hand. Since children often have a hard time mastering the movements to count with their fingers, use the eleven-fingered character as inspiration. First, have children hold up all of their fingers and count to 10. Then, tell children to hold up one finger on their left hands and then one finger on their right hands. Next, instruct them to hold up two fingers on their left hands and then two fingers on their right hands. Continue with three, four, and five fingers on each hand. Practice this a few times, correcting their positions as necessary. Then, make the activity more challenging by having them hold up three fingers on one hand and two on the other. Give them other combinations of numbers to hold up. Practice this for a few minutes each day until children can hold up any number of fingers on either hand with ease.

Gross Motor Connections

Follow Dr. Suess's Directions

There are many motion words in this book. Acting out the words will help children to learn the words' meanings. Take children outside to an open area, read the passages below, and let children act out each of the motion words.

- "They run for fun in the hot, hot, sun."
- "Some are fast."
- "And some are slow."
- "Some are high."
- "And some are low."
- "Just jump on the hump of the Wump of Gump."
- "We saw some sheep take a walk in their sleep."
- "All he does is yell, yell, yell."
- "I hop from left to right and then . . . Hop! Hop! I hop right back again."
- "Did you ever fly a kite in bed?"
- "Did you ever walk with ten cats on your head?"

Art Connections

My Own Suess-Like Fish

Let children make their own fish to celebrate reading the book. Enlarge the Fish Patterns (page 86) for each child. Provide traditional art supplies but also provide materials children can use to make scales, such as small leaves (real or artificial), small circles or triangles cut from different types of paper (tissue, foil, construction paper, etc.), buttons, hole-punch scraps, and more. Also, provide wiggly eyes for children to attach to the fish patterns.

Post the fish on a bulletin board with a blue background. In heavy, black letters, write descriptors similar to the ones written in the book next to the fish. Make sure each fish has a different descriptive phrase.

Creative Dramatics Connections

Phone Manners

There are two different sections in the book where characters are talking on the telephone. One scene shows a friend or relative talking to a crabby character who does not like his bed. The other shows two annoyed characters who cannot hear each other over the phone. Let children practice their phone manners. Provide as many toy phones as possible, or real phones that are no longer in use, as well as pads of paper and pencils to use for taking messages. You can also make some phones that are tin-cans-and-yarn contraptions like the old-fashioned phones shown in the book. Spend some time talking with children on the phones as you teach them important telephone etiquette, such as how to say hello, how to take a message, how and when to dial 9-1-1, and so on. Help children memorize their home phone numbers. Finally, make sure that children understand they should not answer their home phones without parental permission.

Caterpillars and Feet Patterns
Directions are found on page 83.

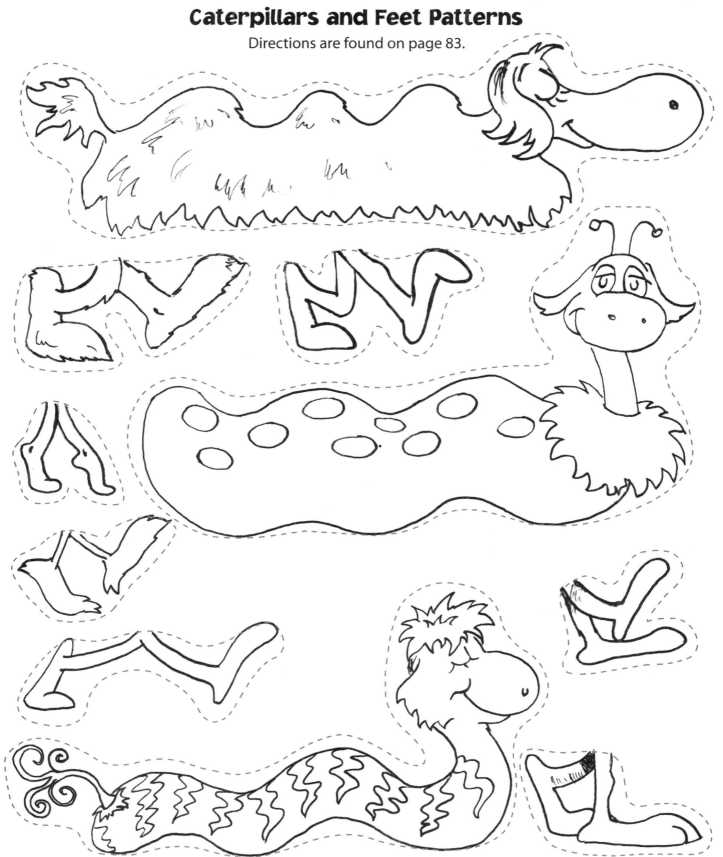

Fish Patterns

Directions are found on page 84.

THE POLAR EXPRESS

Written and illustrated
by Chris Van Allsburg
Copyright 1985, Houghton Mifflin

Story Summary

A boy's belief in Santa is rewarded with a trip to the North Pole. As the recipient of the first gift of Christmas, he asks for a jingle bell from the reindeers' harnesses. After he loses the bell through a hole in his pocket, Santa wraps it and places it under the tree. Even though other adults cannot hear the bell, he is able to hear it for the rest of his life because he is a true believer in Santa.

Themes:
- Christmas
- travel
- gift giving and receiving

Skills:
- sound discrimination
- estimation
- map skills
- geography

Vocabulary:
conductor, harnesses, insisted, lurch, outstretched, rustle, scrape, wilderness

Related Books:
The Night Before Christmas
by Clement Clark Moore
(Running Press, 2001)

Harold at the North Pole
by Crockett Johnson
(HarperTrophy, 2004)

Before the Story

Bring a variety of bells to class and let children take turns shaking them. Ask children to vote on which bell has the most magical sound. Ring the bells as a sound effect when you get to the part of the story that mentions bells.

During the Story

Listening is a very important element in this story. If possible, provide some other sound effects for children to listen to in addition to the bells, such as a train whistle, Christmas caroling, hissing steam, and squeaking metal.

After the Story

You may want to avoid a discussion about belief in Santa Claus. If you think it is safe to risk it, ask children why adults cannot hear the bell in the story, but children can. Also, talk with children about the Christmas gifts Santa has brought them in the past.

Language Arts Connections

The Sounds of Bells

Learning to discriminate sounds is a very important part of learning fluency and pronunciation. Use bells to work on sound discrimination. Record the sounds of several different types of bells, one at a time. Place the recording and the bells at a listening center. Let each child play the recording and then the bells. Have children try to put the bells in the same order as they are heard on the recording.

Singing

Singing is a good fluency activity because it is easier to sing words fluently than speak them. For a fun fluency activity, teach children some Christmas carols. If your school does not encourage religious songs, stick to secular songs, such as "Deck the Halls" (a particularly good choice because of the *fa-la-las*), "We Wish You a Merry Christmas," "Jingle Bells," "Silver Bells," and "Sleigh Ride."

Math Connections

Counting and Then Hot Chocolate

As the train nears the center of the city at the North Pole, the children see "hundreds of elves." But, how do they know what hundreds looks like? Could it have been thousands, or just barely a hundred? Challenge children to visually estimate numbers using the popular estimation guessing game. Fill jars with different numbers of miniature marshmallows: 1, 5, 10, 50, and 100. Gather a small group of children and invite each child to guess how many marshmallows are in each jar. After all children have guessed, reveal the numbers. Then, alter the activity slightly by changing the numbers of marshmallows to 2, 7, 30, 75, and 120. Instead of placing the marshmallows in jars, place them on plastic plates and ask children to estimate the number on each plate. Reveal the actual numbers. Then, make instant hot chocolate, add some new marshmallows, and enjoy a treat with children just like the children enjoyed on the train.

Science Connections

Topographic Map

As a class project, create a topographic map based on descriptions of the train ride. Use a large sheet of cardboard, painted white, for the base. Gather green chenille craft sticks (cut in half), cardboard egg cartons (cut into sections), strips of heavy white paper, white glue or flour and salt, and water. On the cardboard, let children mark off areas for the forest, mountains, and plains. Push the ends of the chenille craft sticks through the cardboard, bending the ends underneath, to create a forest.

Glue stacks of egg carton cups to the base to create mountains. Then, make one of the Papier-Mâché Recipes (page 90). Let children dip paper strips into the mixture and cover the flat and mountainous parts of the map. When the map is dry, draw on train tracks. Add plastic animals to the forest and plastic buildings to represent the village. Finally, spray the entire map with hair spray or add a thin coating of the papier-mâché mixture; then, let children sprinkle salt on the map to make it sparkle with "snow."

Problem-Solving and Social Skills Connections

The Joy of Giving a Gift

If the children in your classroom celebrate Christmas or any other gift-giving occasion, help them experience the joy that comes with giving a gift. Ask children to talk about how the boy felt receiving the first gift of Christmas and how they have felt receiving gifts in the past. Then, do a family gift-giving project with children. Provide a large spool of elastic cord, several bags of jingle bells, and some decorative ribbon. Cut a length of elastic cord about 7" (18 cm) long for each child. Wrap tape around one end to make a point for lacing. Tie the other end of the elastic to a paper clip. Let each child string jingle bells onto the elastic cord until it is full but not too stretched. Twist the two ends together and knot. Let each child use ribbon to tie a bow around the elastic. Before letting children give the wreaths as gifts, complete the Fine Motor Connections activity (page 89).

Fine Motor Connections

Wrapping a Special Gift

One of the most special parts of this book is when the boy unwraps his gift from Santa. Use gift wrap to help children practice fine motor skills. Stock a craft box with wrapping paper, tape, empty boxes large enough to hold a small wreath (see the Problem-Solving and Social Skills Connections activity, page 88), and ribbon. If children can use scissors, include them with the wrapping paper; otherwise, precut sheets of wrapping paper. Spend time with children in small groups and teach them to cut the paper to the correct size, fold it around the boxes, tape it in place, and finish with ribbons. If children have made wreaths for gifts in the Problem-Solving and Social Skills activity, let them wrap their gifts in this activity. After children have given their gifts, have them draw pictures of giving their gifts and the reactions they received. Ask children to describe how giving the gifts made them feel.

Gross Motor Connections

Going on a Train Trip

Recapture the excitement of the train's trip through the mountains. Provide two lengths of rope that are about 10' (3 m) long. (Adjust the lengths of the ropes according to the number of children in the classroom.) Have children form a line. Place the lengths of rope on either side of the line and tell children to pick them up, holding one rope in each hand. Now that children are connected by the rope, explain that they are connected like the cars on a train. Lead the "train" though the hallway, upstairs, around the playground, and if possible, up and down hills. Challenge children to stay together, just like train cars. Then, designate one child to lead the train. If any children let the train fall apart, call out, "Off the track!" Have children who fall off the track go to the back of the train line. Give each child an opportunity to be the engine (in the front) and the caboose (in the back).

Art Connections

Our Own Polar Express Village

Chris Van Allsburg describes the narrator's final destination as "a huge city standing alone at the top of the world, filled with factories where every Christmas toy was made." Obtain several strands of white lights. Ask each child to bring a box (any size) from home. Let children draw windows and doors on the boxes and decorate them to look like toy factories.

If possible, provide small, plastic toys for children to glue to the boxes to create signs to show which toys are made inside. Use candy wafers, cinnamon candies, or other small objects to make roof shingles. After children have left for the day, use a craft knife to cut out some of the doors and windows children have drawn. Gather the decorated boxes together and arrange them to look like a city. If possible, place them in a large closet or an area that can be darkened during the daytime. Arrange the lights so that each building has a few inside, plug them in, and dim the room lights so that children can see the city when they arrive at school the next morning.

Creative Dramatics Connections

Up, Up, and Away in a Sleigh

Use the buildings created in the Art Connections activity (left) to inspire dramatic play. After you have displayed the city with the lights, move the buildings apart and place them on a few chairs in a small area on the floor. Provide a few strands of jingle bells and a few prewrapped presents and place them in an appliance box to create a sleigh.

Let children take turns pretending they are Santa and his reindeer flying high over the city on Christmas Eve. To add to the fun, make a fireplace from cardboard and hang stockings from it using clothespins. Provide wrapped candies, small toys, and other goodies in a cloth sack. Let children get out of the cardboard box sleigh and fill the stockings with the goodies from the bag.

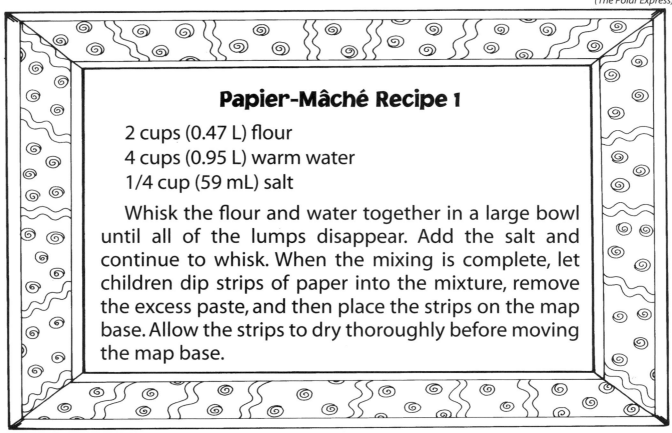

Papier-Mâché Recipe 1

2 cups (0.47 L) flour
4 cups (0.95 L) warm water
1/4 cup (59 mL) salt

Whisk the flour and water together in a large bowl until all of the lumps disappear. Add the salt and continue to whisk. When the mixing is complete, let children dip strips of paper into the mixture, remove the excess paste, and then place the strips on the map base. Allow the strips to dry thoroughly before moving the map base.

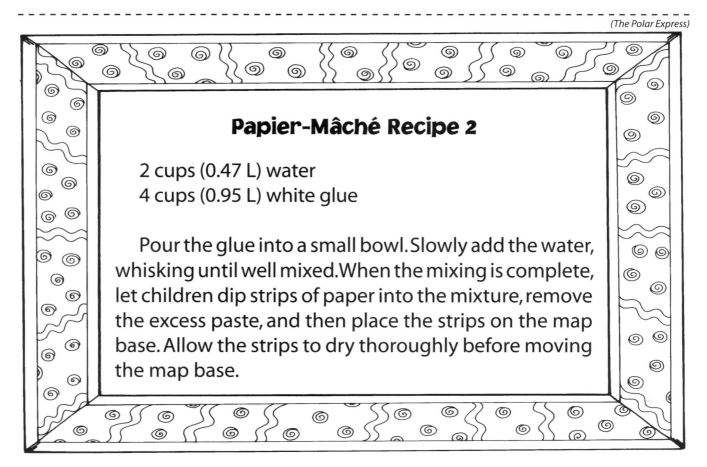

Papier-Mâché Recipe 2

2 cups (0.47 L) water
4 cups (0.95 L) white glue

Pour the glue into a small bowl. Slowly add the water, whisking until well mixed. When the mixing is complete, let children dip strips of paper into the mixture, remove the excess paste, and then place the strips on the map base. Allow the strips to dry thoroughly before moving the map base.

(The Polar Express)

First Gift of Christmas

Directions: Pretend you have been chosen to receive the first gift of Christmas. You can choose any gift from Santa. What will you choose? Draw a picture of the gift in the box.

Creating Curriculum Using Children's Picture Books - 91 -

THE THREE PIGS

Written and illustrated
by David Wiesner
Copyright 2001
Clarion Books

Story Summary

In this delightful alternative to the traditional fairy tale, the three pigs escape the story. Their explorations take them to a nursery rhyme and an adventure story, where they rescue the cat and his fiddle and a doomed dragon. In the end, the pigs and their new companions return to the brick house and live happily ever after, of course. Some things, luckily, never change.

Themes:
- storytelling
- fairy tales
- imagination

Skills:
- dialogue construction
- number sentences
- physics

Vocabulary:
determined, eldest, fiddle, fortune, guard, methinks, sport, steed, swine

Related Books:
Three Little Pigs
by Golden Books
(Golden/Disney, 2004)

Three Little Pigs
by James Marshall
(Grosset & Dunlap, 2000)

Hey, Diddle, Diddle!
by Salley Mavor
(Houghton Mifflin, 2005)

Before the Story

Read a traditional version of the story of the three pigs and talk about what happens to the pigs. (Sometimes they get eaten and sometimes each pig simply escapes and moves to the next pig's house.) Talk about how the first two pigs might have saved their houses.

During the Story

It is easy for children to become confused with this version of the story since so many unexpected things happen. In addition, several of the pages have no text and their illustrations are from unusual perspectives. Pause at these pages to talk at length about what is happening to the pigs, where they are going, and why the art styles change as the story changes.

After the Story

Do a step-by-step comparison of two versions of this fairy tale to help children understand the unique story device used by the author. Have a volunteer hold a traditional version of the story of the three pigs and turn its pages. Follow the story line simultaneously in each book and compare the pages of the traditional book to the folded pages in Wiesner's version after the pigs escape. Ask children to point out what is happening in the folded pages using the traditional book as a reference.

Language Arts Connections

Retell the Story

The Three Little Pigs has always been a favorite children's story. Let children enjoy retelling the story using flannel board characters. Copy the Pigs, House, and Wolf Patterns (pages 95 and 96.) Color the patterns, cut them out, and laminate them for durability. Place the "loop" side of self-stick hook-and-loop tape on the back of each character. The children will spend hours giggling and making up creative new versions of this traditional tale.

Math Connections

Little Pig Math

Copy, color, cut out, and laminate at least 20 of the Pigs Patterns (page 95). Place the "loop" side of self-stick hook-and-loop tape or self-stick magnetic tape on the back of each pig. Also, prepare the following math symbols and number cards: numerals 1 through 10 and +, −, and = symbols. Let children use these to create simple math sentences such as:

Or, simply place little pigs on the flannel board. Have the children count the pigs and then place the correct number card next to the pigs.

Science Connections

Flying Pigs!

Do a high-flying experiment. Give each child a copy of the Paper Airplane Pattern (page 95) and the Three Little Pigs Patterns (page 95). Help each child cut out one set of pig patterns and one airplane. Fold the airplane in half along line number 1 and then finish folding the plane according to the numbers along each line.

Have children guess how the planes will fly best—with zero, one, two, or three pigs attached. Let children fly their planes without any pig passengers. As children are flying their planes, draw and label four columns on the board: "Zero Pigs," "One Pig," "Two Pigs," and "Three Pigs." Have children describe how the planes flew without passengers. Record some of the responses. Then, help each child tape one pig to the plane. Allow children to fly the planes again and record the results. Repeat for the remaining two pigs. Finally, discuss which number of passengers gave the best flying results. If children are old enough, explain that adding the paper pigs created extra weight and wind resistance, which made it harder for the planes to fly.

Problem-Solving and Social Skills Connections

Help the Pigs and the Wolf Become Friends

The three clever pigs are able to escape the wolf, but perhaps, there could be another way to deal with him. Provide stuffed animal pigs and a stuffed animal wolf. Assign children to groups of four and let the groups play one at a time. Give an animal to each child. Ask children to think about other ways the pigs and the wolf could have ended the story without the pigs being eaten and their houses being destroyed. Inspire children by asking what the wolf wanted.

Was he just being mean or was there another reason for the things he did? If children can figure out that he was hungry, help them think of ways the pigs and wolf could have worked together so that the wolf was no longer hungry, the houses remained intact, and the pigs did not get eaten.

Fine Motor Connections

Retell the Story with Props

Let children use simple materials to recreate the story of the three pigs. Locate a small set of plastic farm animals that includes three pigs and a wolf, if possible. Gather small milk cartons, rinse them thoroughly, and then use a craft knife to cut a hole in each. The holes should be larger than the animal figures. Provide each child with three of the milk cartons, glue, straw, twigs, and red paper squares. (You can also cut erasers into small rectangles to make "bricks.") Let each child use glue to carefully attach the various materials to the milk cartons to create the three different houses. After the houses are dry, give each child access to the pigs and the wolf and let children sort the pigs into their houses as they retell the story.

Gross Motor Connections

Brick Relay Races

Show children the title page where the three pigs are transporting their house-building materials to their building sites. Ask, "How did the pigs get the sticks and wood on their backs and load the bricks in the wagon if they do not have any hands?" Supply "bricks" (cardboard blocks or large car washing sponges) and three children's wagons for a no-hands race. Separate the bricks into equal piles and assign children to three teams. Tell children that they must race to get the bricks into the wagons without using their hands at all. Also, clarify that they may not use their teeth, for sanitary reasons. When you say, "Go!" children can work together or individually using their feet and knees to get the bricks into the wagons, but they must fold their arms behind their backs and keep them there at all times. Reward all players with "straw" (Chinese noodles), "sticks" (stick pretzels), and "bricks" (red gelatin cut into small rectangles) for snack.

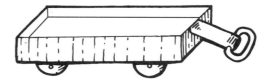

Art Connections

Paper Bag Pigs and Wolves

Provide each child with two small, lunch-size paper bags and construction paper in the following colors: pink, black, white, and brown. To make a pig, each child should cut out a pink paper circle for a nose, drawing two small black circles for nostrils. Then, cut two pink triangles for ears and two white circles for eyes, drawing black pupils on the eyes. Glue all of the pieces onto a paper bag. Finally, draw a mouth on the bag to complete the pig.

To make a wolf, cut out a long, thin brown paper triangle and a small black circle. Glue the circle to the end of the triangle for the wolf's nose. Cut out brown triangles for ears and white circles for eyes, drawing black pupils on the eyes. Glue all of the pieces onto a paper bag. Finally, draw a mouth on the bag and perhaps a few shiny teeth.

Creative Dramatics Connections

Our Own Straw, Stick, and Brick Houses

Children will love making a huge commotion in the classroom. Ask parents to donate large boxes (cereal boxes or larger). You will need at least 50 boxes for this activity. If possible, also acquire boxes from an appliance store. Cut yellow and brown butcher paper into strips. Glue the yellow strips (straw) to half of the cereal size boxes and brown strips (sticks) to the other half. Then, cut doors in the appliance boxes and paint them dark red to look like bricks. Let children take turns being the wolves and pigs. One child can build a house (a wall to crouch behind) from the "straw," one can build with the "sticks," and one can hide inside the box painted to look like bricks. Let the child who is playing the wolf try to blow down (or knock down) the straw house, then the house of sticks, and finally the brick house. The children who are playing the pigs can run from house to house if they do not wish to be eaten.

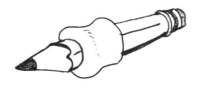

Paper Airplane Pattern
Directions are found on page 93.

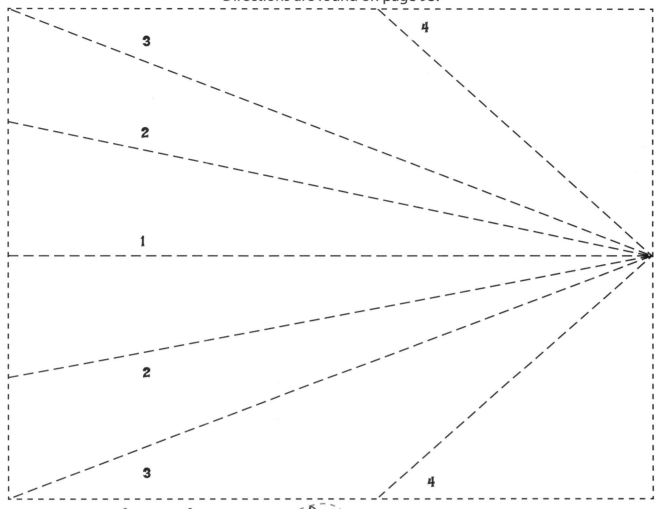

3

4

2

1

2

3

4

The Three Little Pigs Patterns

Directions are found on page 93.

House and Wolf Patterns
Directions are found on page 93.

Creating Curriculum Using Children's Picture Books